Memoirs of Casanova Volume VII

Memoirs of Casanova Volume VII

Giacomo Casanova

MINT EDITIONS

Memoirs of Casanova Volume VII was first published in 1902.

This edition published by Mint Editions 2021.

ISBN 9781513281896 | E-ISBN 9781513286914

Published by Mint Editions®

**MINT
EDITIONS**

minteditionbooks.com

Publishing Director: Jennifer Newens
Design & Production: Rachel Lopez Metzger
Project Manager: Micaela Clark
Translated By: Arthur Machen
Typesetting: Westchester Publishing Services

Contents

I

Arrived, for the first time, in the capital of Austria, at the age of eight-and-twenty, well provided with clothes, but rather short of money—a circumstance which made it necessary for me to curtail my expenses until the arrival of the proceeds of a letter of exchange which I had drawn upon M. de Bragadin. The only letter of recommendation I had was from the poet Migliavacca, of Dresden, addressed to the illustrious Abbe Metastasio, whom I wished ardently to know. I delivered the letter the day after my arrival, and in one hour of conversation I found him more learned than I should have supposed from his works. Besides, Metastasio was so modest that at first I did not think that modesty natural, but it was not long before I discovered that it was genuine, for when he recited something of his own composition, he was the first to call the attention of his hearers to the important parts or to the fine passages with as much simplicity as he would remark the weak ones. I spoke to him of his tutor Gravina, and as we were on that subject he recited to me five or six stanzas which he had written on his death, and which had not been printed. Moved by the remembrance of his friend, and by the sad beauty of his own poetry, his eyes were filled with tears, and when he had done reciting the stanzas he said, in a tone of touching simplicity,'Ditemi il vero, si puo air meglio'?

I answered that he alone had the right to believe it impossible. I then asked him whether he had to work a great deal to compose his beautiful poetry; he shewed me four or five pages which he had covered with erasures and words crossed and scratched out only because he had wished to bring fourteen lines to perfection, and he assured me that he had never been able to compose more than that number in one day. He confirmed my knowledge of a truth which I had found out before, namely, that the very lines which most readers believe to have flowed easily from the poet's pen are generally those which he has had the greatest difficulty in composing.

"Which of your operas," I enquired, "do you like best?"

"'Attilio Regolo; ma questo non vuol gia dire che sia il megliore'."

"All your works have been translated in Paris into French prose, but the publisher was ruined, for it is not possible to read them, and it proves the elevation and the power of your poetry."

"Several years ago, another foolish publisher ruined himself by a translation into French prose of the splendid poetry of Ariosto. I laugh at those who maintain that poetry can be translated into prose."

"I am of your opinion."

"And you are right."

He told me that he had never written an arietta without composing the music of it himself, but that as a general rule he never shewed his music to anyone.

"The French," he added, "entertain the very strange belief that it is possible to adapt poetry to music already composed."

And he made on that subject this very philosophical remark:

"You might just as well say to a sculptor, 'Here is a piece of marble, make a Venus, and let her expression be shewn before the features are chiselled.'"

I went to the Imperial Library, and was much surprised to meet De la Haye in the company of two Poles, and a young Venetian whom his father had entrusted to him to complete his education. I believed him to be in Poland, and as the meeting recalled interesting recollections I was pleased to see him. I embraced him repeatedly with real pleasure.

He told me that he was in Vienna on business, and that he would go to Venice during the summer. We paid one another several visits, and hearing that I was rather short of money he lent me fifty ducats, which I returned a short time after. He told me that Bavois was already lieutenant-colonel in the Venetian army, and the news afforded me great pleasure. He had been fortunate enough to be appointed adjutant-general by M. Morosini, who, after his return from his embassy in France, had made him Commissary of the Borders. I was delighted to hear of the happiness and success of two men who certainly could not help acknowledging me as the original cause of their good fortune. In Vienna I acquired the certainty of De la Haye being a Jesuit, but he would not let anyone allude to the subject.

Not knowing where to go, and longing for some recreation, I went to the rehearsal of the opera which was to be performed after Easter, and met Bodin, the first dancer, who had married the handsome Jeoffroi, whom I had seen in Turin. I likewise met in the same place Campioni, the husband of the beautiful Ancilla. He told me that he had been compelled to apply for a divorce because she dishonoured him too publicly. Campioni was at the same time a great dancer and a great gambler. I took up my lodgings with him.

In Vienna everything is beautiful; money was then very plentiful, and luxury very great; but the severity of the empress made the worship of Venus difficult, particularly for strangers. A legion of vile spies, who were decorated with the fine title of Commissaries of Chastity, were the merciless tormentors of all the girls. The empress did not practise the sublime virtue of tolerance for what is called illegitimate love, and in her excessive devotion she thought that her persecutions of the most natural inclinations in man and woman were very agreeable to God. Holding in her imperial hands the register of cardinal sins, she fancied that she could be indulgent for six of them, and keep all her severity for the seventh, lewdness, which in her estimation could not be forgiven.

"One can ignore pride," she would say, "for dignity wears the same garb. Avarice is fearful, it is true; but one might be mistaken about it, because it is often very like economy. As for anger, it is a murderous disease in its excess, but murder is punishable with death. Gluttony is sometimes nothing but epicurism, and religion does not forbid that sin; for in good company it is held a valuable quality; besides, it blends itself with appetite, and so much the worse for those who die of indigestion. Envy is a low passion which no one ever avows; to punish it in any other way than by its own corroding venom, I would have to torture everybody at Court; and weariness is the punishment of sloth. But lust is a different thing altogether; my chaste soul could not forgive such a sin, and I declare open war against it. My subjects are at liberty to think women handsome as much as they please; women may do all in their power to appear beautiful; people may entertain each other as they like, because I cannot forbid conversation; but they shall not gratify desires on which the preservation of the human race depends, unless it is in the holy state of legal marriage. Therefore, all the miserable creatures who live by the barter of their caresses and of the charms given to them by nature shall be sent to Temeswar. I am aware that in Rome people are very indulgent on that point, and that, in order to prevent another greater crime (which is not prevented), every cardinal has one or more mistresses, but in Rome the climate requires certain concessions which are not necessary here, where the bottle and the pipe replace all pleasures. (She might have added, and the table, for the Austrians are known to be terrible eaters.)

"I will have no indulgence either for domestic disorders, for the moment I hear that a wife is unfaithful to her husband, I will have her locked up, in spite of all, in spite of the generally received opinion that the husband is the real judge and master of his wife; that privilege cannot be granted in my kingdom where husbands are by far too indifferent on that subject. Fanatic husbands may complain as much as they please that I dishonour them by punishing their wives; they are dishonoured already by the fact of the woman's infidelity."

"But, madam, dishonour rises in reality only from the fact of infidelity being made public; besides, you might be deceived, although you are empress."

"I know that, but that is no business of yours, and I do not grant you the right of contradicting me."

Such is the way in which Maria Teresa would have argued, and notwithstanding the principle of virtue from which her argument had originated, it had ultimately given birth to all the infamous deeds which her executioners, the Commissaries of Chastity, committed with impunity under her name. At every hour of the day, in all the streets of Vienna, they carried off and took to prison the poor girls who happened to live alone, and very often went out only to earn an honest living. I should like to know how it was possible to know that a girl was going to some man to get from him consolations for her miserable position, or that she was in search of someone disposed to offer her those consolations? Indeed, it was difficult. A spy would follow them at a distance. The police department kept a crowd of those spies, and as the scoundrels wore no particular uniform, it was impossible to know them; as a natural consequence, there was a general distrust of all strangers. If a girl entered a house, the spy who had followed her, waited for her, stopped her as she came out, and subjected her to an interrogatory. If the poor creature looked uneasy, if she hesitated in answering in such a way as to satisfy the spy, the fellow would take her to prison; in all cases beginning by plundering her of whatever money or jewellery she carried about her person, and the restitution of which could never be obtained. Vienna was, in that respect a true den of privileged thieves. It happened to me one day in Leopoldstadt that in the midst of some tumult a girl slipped in my hand a gold watch to secure it from the clutches of a police-spy who was pressing upon her to take her up. I did not know the poor girl, whom I was fortunate enough to see again one month afterwards. She was pretty, and she had been compelled to more than one sacrifice in order to obtain her liberty. I was glad to be able to hand her watch back to her, and although she was well worthy of a man's attention I did not ask her for anything to reward my faithfulness.

The only way in which girls could walk unmolested in the streets was to go about with their head bent down with beads in hand, for in that case the disgusting brood of spies dared not arrest them, because they might be on their way to church, and Maria Teresa would certainly have sent to the gallows the spy guilty of such a mistake.

Those low villains rendered a stay in Vienna very unpleasant to foreigners, and it was a matter of the greatest difficulty to gratify the slightest natural want without running the risk of being annoyed. One day as I was standing close to the wall in a narrow street, I was much astonished at hearing myself rudely addressed by a scoundrel with a round wig, who told me that, if I did not go somewhere else to finish what I had begun, he would have me arrested!

"And why, if you please?"

"Because, on your left, there is a woman who can see you."

I lifted up my head, and I saw on the fourth story, a woman who, with the telescope she had applied to her eye, could have told whether I was a Jew or a Christian. I obeyed, laughing heartily, and related the adventure everywhere; but no one was astonished, because the same thing happened over and over again every day.

In order to study the manners and habits of the people, I took my meals in all sorts of places. One day, having gone with Campioni to dine at "The Crawfish," I found, to my great surprise, sitting at the table d'hote, that Pepe il Cadetto, whose acquaintance I had made at the time of my arrest in the Spanish army, and whom I had met afterwards in Venice and in Lyons, under the name of Don Joseph Marcati. Campioni, who had been his partner in Lyons, embraced him, talked with him in private, and informed me that the man had resumed his real name, and that he was now called Count Afflisio. He told me that after dinner there would be a faro bank in which I would have an interest, and he therefore requested me not to play. I accepted the offer. Afflisio won: a captain of the name of Beccaxia threw the cards at his face—a trifle to which the self-styled count was accustomed, and which did not elicit any remark from him. When the game was over, we repaired to the coffee-room, where an officer of gentlemanly appearance, staring at me, began to smile, but not in an offensive manner.

"Sir," I asked him, politely, "may I ask why you are laughing?"

"It makes me laugh to see that you do not recognize me."

"I have some idea that I have seen you somewhere, but I could not say where or when I had that honour."

"Nine years ago, by the orders of the Prince de Lobkowitz, I escorted you to the Gate of Rimini."

"You are Baron Vais."

"Precisely."

We embraced one another; he offered me his friendly services, promising to procure me all the pleasure he could in Vienna. I accepted gratefully, and the same evening he presented me to a countess, at whose house I made the acquaintance of the Abbe Testagrossa, who was called Grosse-Tete by everybody. He was minister of the Duke of Modem, and great at Court because he had negotiated the marriage of the arch-duke with Beatrice d'Este. I also became acquainted there with the Count of Roquendorf and Count Sarotin, and with several noble young ladies who are called in Germany frauleins, and with a baroness who had led a pretty wild life, but who could yet captivate a man. We had supper, and I was created baron. It was in vain that I observed that I had no title whatever: "You must be something," I was told, "and you cannot be less than baron. You must confess yourself to be at least that, if you wish to be received anywhere in Vienna."

"Well, I will be a baron, since it is of no importance."

The baroness was not long before she gave me to understand that she felt kindly disposed towards me, and that she would receive my attentions with pleasure; I paid her a visit the very next day. "If you are fond of cards," she said, "come in the evening." At her house I made the acquaintance of several gamblers, and of three or four frauleins who, without any dread of the Commissaries of Chastity, were devoted to the worship of Venus, and were so kindly disposed that they were not afraid of lowering their nobility by accepting some reward for their kindness—a circumstance which proved to me that the Commissaries were in the habit of troubling only the girls who did not frequent good houses.

The baroness invited me to introduce, all my friends, so I brought to her house Vais, Campioni, and Afflisio. The last one played, held the bank, won; and Tramontini, with whom I had become acquainted, presented him to his wife, who was called Madame Tasi. It was through her that Afflisio made the useful acquaintance of the Prince of Saxe-Hildburghausen. This introduction was the origin of the great fortune made by that contrabrand count, because Tramontini, who had become his partner in all important gambling transactions, contrived to obtain for him from the prince the rank of captain in the service of their imperial and royal majesties, and in less than three weeks Afflisio wore the uniform and the insignia of his grade. When I left Vienna he possessed one: hundred thousand florins. Their majesties were fond of gambling but not of punting. The emperor had a creature of his own to hold the bank. He was a kind, magnificent, but not extravagant, prince. I saw him in his grand imperial costume, and I was surprised to see him dressed in the Spanish fashion. I almost fancied I had before my eyes Charles V of Spain, who had established that etiquette which was still in existence, although after him no emperor had been a Spaniard, and although Francis I. had nothing in common with that nation.

In Poland, some years afterwards, I saw the same caprice at the coronation of Stanislas Augustus Poniatowski, and the old palatine noblemen almost broke their hearts at the sight of that costume; but they had to shew as good a countenance as they could, for under Russian despotism the only privilege they enjoyed was that of resignation.

The Emperor Francis I was, handsome, and would have looked so under the hood of a monk as well as under an imperial crown. He had every possible consideration for his wife, and allowed her to get the state into debt, because he possessed the art of becoming himself the creditor of the state. He favoured commerce because it filled his coffers. He was rather addicted to gallantry, and the empress, who always called him master feigned not to notice it, because she did not want the world to know that her charms could no longer captivate her royal spouse, and the more so that the beauty of her numerous family was generally admired. All the archduchesses except the eldest seemed to me very handsome; but amongst the sons I had the opportunity of seeing only the eldest, and I thought the expression of his face bad and unpleasant, in spite of the contrary opinion of Abbe Grosse-Tete, who prided himself upon being a good physiognomist.

"What do you see," he asked me one day, "on the countenance of that prince?"

"Self-conceit and suicide."

It was a prophecy, for Joseph II positively killed himself, although not wilfully, and it was his self-conceit which prevented him from knowing it. He was not wanting in learning, but the knowledge which he believed himself to possess destroyed the learning which he had in reality. He delighted in speaking to those who did not know how to answer him, whether because they were amazed at his arguments, or because they pretended to be so; but he called pedants, and avoided all persons, who by true reasoning pulled down the weak scaffolding of his arguments. Seven years ago I happened to meet him at Luxemburg, and he spoke to me with just contempt of a man who had exchanged immense sums of money, and a great deal of debasing meanness against some miserable parchments, and he added,—

"I despise men who purchase nobility."

"Your majesty is right, but what are we to think of those who sell it?"

After that question he turned his back upon me, and hence forth he thought me unworthy of being spoken to.

The great passion of that king was to see those who listened to him laugh, whether with sincerity or with affectation, when he related something; he could narrate well and amplify in a very amusing manner all the particulars of an anecdote; but he called anyone who did not laugh at his jests a fool, and that was always the person who understood him best. He gave the preference to the opinion of Brambilla, who encouraged his suicide, over that of the physicians who were directing him according to reason. Nevertheless, no one ever denied his claim to great courage; but he had no idea whatever of the art of government, for he had not the slightest knowledge of the human heart, and he could neither dissemble nor keep a secret; he had so little control over his own countenance that he could not even conceal the pleasure he felt in punishing, and when he saw anyone whose features did not please him, he could not help making a wry face which disfigured him greatly.

Joseph II sank under a truly cruel disease, which left him until the last moment the faculty of arguing upon everything, at the same time that he knew his death to be certain. This prince must have felt the misery of repenting everything he had done and of seeing the impossibility of undoing it, partly because it was irreparable, partly because if he had undone through reason what he had done through senselessness, he would have thought himself dishonoured, for he must have clung to the last to the belief of the infallibility attached to his high birth, in spite of the state of languor of his soul which ought to have proved to him the weakness and the fallibility of his nature. He had the greatest esteem for his brother, who has now succeeded him, but he had not the courage to follow the advice which that brother gave him. An impulse worthy of a great soul made him bestow a large reward upon the physician, a man of intelligence, who pronounced his sentence of death, but a completely opposite weakness had prompted him, a few months before, to load with benefits the doctors and the quack who made him believe that they had cured him. He must likewise have felt the misery of knowing that he would not be regretted after his death—a grievous thought, especially for a sovereign. His niece, whom he loved dearly, died before him, and, if he had had the affection of those who surrounded him, they would have spared him that fearful information, for it was evident that his end was near at hand, and no one could dread his anger for having kept that event from him.

Although very much pleased with Vienna and with the pleasures I enjoyed with the beautiful frauleins, whose acquaintance I had made at the house of the baroness, I was thinking of leaving that agreeable city, when Baron Vais, meeting me at Count Durazzo's wedding, invited me to join a picnic at Schoenbrunn. I went, and I failed to observe the laws of temperance; the consequence was that I returned to Vienna with such a severe indigestion that in twenty-four hours I was at the point of death.

I made use of the last particle of intelligence left in me by the disease to save my own life. Campioni, Roquendorf and Sarotin were by my bedside. M. Sarotin, who felt great friendship for me, had brought a physician, although I had almost positively declared that I would not see one. That disciple of Sangrado, thinking that he could allow full sway to the despotism of science, had sent for a surgeon, and they were going to bleed me against my will. I was half-dead; I do not know by what strange inspiration I opened my eyes, and I saw a man, standing lancet in hand and preparing to open the vein.

"No, no!" I said.

And I languidly withdrew my arm; but the tormentor wishing, as the physician expressed it, to restore me to life in spite of myself, got hold of my arm again. I suddenly felt my strength returning. I put my hand forward, seized one of my pistols, fired, and the ball cut off one of the locks of his hair. That was enough; everybody ran away, with the exception of my servant, who did not abandon me, and gave me as much water as I wanted to drink. On the fourth day I had recovered my usual good health.

That adventure amused all the idlers of Vienna for several days, and Abbe Grosse-Tete assured me that if I had killed the poor surgeon, it would not have gone any further, because all the witnesses present in my room at the time would have declared that he wanted to use violence to bleed me, which made it a case of legitimate self-defence. I was likewise told by several persons that all the physicians in Vienna were of opinion that if I had been bled I should have been a dead man; but if drinking water had not saved me, those gentlemen would certainly not have expressed the same opinion. I felt, however, that I had to be careful, and not to fall ill in the capital of Austria, for it was likely that I should not have found a physician without difficulty. At the opera, a great many persons wished after that to make my acquaintance, and I was looked upon as a man who had fought, pistol in hand, against death. A miniature-painter named Morol, who was subject to indigestions and who was at last killed by one, had taught me his system which was that, to cure those attacks, all that was necessary was to drink plenty of water and to be patient. He died because he was bled once when he could not oppose any resistance.

My indigestion reminded me of a witty saying of a man who was not much in the habit of uttering many of them; I mean M. de Maisonrouge, who was taken home one day almost dying from a severe attack of indigestion: his carriage having been stopped opposite the Quinze-Vingts by some obstruction, a poor man came up and begged alms, saying,

"Sir, I am starving."

"Eh! what are you complaining of?" answered Maisonrouge, sighing deeply; "I wish I was in your place, you rogue!"

At that time I made the acquaintance of a Milanese dancer, who had wit, excellent manners, a literary education, and what is more—great beauty. She received very good society, and did the honours of her drawing-room marvellously well. I became acquainted at her house with Count Christopher Erdodi, an amiable, wealthy and generous man; and with a certain Prince Kinski who had all the grace of a harlequin. That girl inspired me with love, but it was in vain, for she was herself enamoured of a dancer from Florence, called Argiolini. I courted her, but she only laughed at me, for an actress, if in love with someone, is a fortress which cannot be taken, unless you build a bridge of gold, and I was not rich. Yet I did not despair, and kept on burning my incense at her feet. She liked my society because she used to shew me the letters she wrote, and I was very careful to admire her style. She had her own portrait in miniature, which was an excellent likeness. The day before my departure, vexed at having lost my time and my amorous compliments, I made up my mind to steal that portrait—a slight compensation for not having won the original. As I was taking leave of her, I saw the portrait within my reach, seized it, and left Vienna for Presburg, where Baron Vais had invited me to accompany him and several lovely frauleins on a party of pleasure.

When we got out of the carriages, the first person I tumbled upon was the Chevalier de Talvis, the protector of Madame Conde-Labre, whom I had treated so well in Paris. The moment he saw me, he came up and told me that I owed him his revenge.

"I promise to give it to you, but I never leave one pleasure for another," I answered; "we shall see one another again."

"That is enough. Will you do me the honour to introduce me to these ladies?"

"Very willingly, but not in the street."

We went inside of the hotel and he followed us. Thinking that the man, who after all was as brave as a French chevalier, might amuse us, I presented him to my friends. He had been staying at the same hotel for a couple of days, and he was in mourning. He asked us if we intended to go to the prince-bishop's ball; it was the first news we had of it. Vais answered affirmatively.

"One can attend it," said Talvis, "without being presented, and that is why we intend to go, for I am not known to anybody here."

He left us, and the landlord, having come in to receive our orders, gave us some particulars respecting the ball. Our lovely frauleins expressing a wish to attend it, we made up our minds to gratify them.

We were not known to anyone, and were rambling through the apartments, when we arrived before a large table at which the prince-bishop was holding a faro bank. The pile of gold that the noble prelate had before him could not have been less than thirteen or fourteen thousand florins. The Chevalier de Talvis was standing between two ladies to whom he was whispering sweet words, while the prelate was shuffling the cards.

The prince, looking at the chevalier, took it into his head to ask him, in a most engaging manner to risk a card.

"Willingly, my lord," said Talvis; "the whole of the bank upon this card."

"Very well," answered the prelate, to shew that he was not afraid.

He dealt, Talvis won, and my lucky Frenchman, with the greatest coolness, filled his pockets with the prince's gold. The bishop, astonished, and seeing but rather late how foolish he had been, said to the chevalier,

"Sir, if you had lost, how would you have managed to pay me?"

"My lord, that is my business."

"You are more lucky than wise."

"Most likely, my lord; but that is my business."

Seeing that the chevalier was on the point of leaving, I followed him, and at the bottom of the stairs, after congratulating him, I asked him to lend me a hundred sovereigns. He gave them to me at once, assuring me that he was delighted to have it in his power to oblige me.

"I will give you my bill."

"Nothing of the sort."

I put the gold into my pocket, caring very little for the crowd of masked persons whom curiosity had brought around the lucky winner, and who had witnessed the transaction. Talvis went away, and I returned to the ball-room.

Roquendorf and Sarotin, who were amongst the guests, having heard that the chevalier had handed me some gold, asked me who he was. I gave them an answer half true and half false, and I told them that the gold I had just received was the payment of a sum I had lent him in Paris. Of course they could not help believing me, or at least pretending to do so.

When we returned to the inn, the landlord informed us that the chevalier had left the city on horseback, as fast as he could gallop, and that a small traveling-bag was all his luggage. We sat down to supper, and in order to make our meal more cheerful, I told Vais and our charming frauleins the manner in which I had known Talvis, and how I had contrived to have my share of what he had won.

On our arrival in Vienna, the adventure was already known; people admired the Frenchman and laughed at the bishop. I was not spared by public rumour, but I took no notice of it, for I did not think it necessary to defend myself. No one knew the Chevalier de Talvis, and the French ambassador was not even acquainted with his name. I do not know whether he was ever heard of again.

I left Vienna in a post-chaise, after I had said farewell to my friends, ladies and gentlemen, and on the fourth day I slept in Trieste. The next day I sailed for Venice, which I reached in the afternoon, two days before Ascension Day. After an absence of three years I had the happiness of embracing my beloved protector, M. de Bragadin, and his two inseparable friends, who were delighted to see me in good health and well equipped.

II

I Return the Portrait I Had Stolen in Vienna I
Proceed to Padua; An Adventure on My Way Back, and
Its Consequences—I Meet Therese Imer Again—My
Acquaintance With Mademoiselle C. C.

I found myself again in my native country with that feeling of delight which is experienced by all true-hearted men, when they see again the place in which they have received the first lasting impressions. I had acquired some experience; I knew the laws of honour and politeness; in one word, I felt myself superior to most of my equals, and I longed to resume my old habits and pursuits; but I intended to adopt a more regular and more reserved line of conduct.

I saw with great pleasure, as I entered my study, the perfect 'statu quo' which had been preserved there. My papers, covered with a thick layer of dust, testified well enough that no strange hand had ever meddled with them.

Two days after my arrival, as I was getting ready to accompany the Bucentoro, on which the Doge was going, as usual, to wed the Adriatic, the widow of so many husbands, and yet as young as on the first day of her creation, a gondolier brought me a letter. It was from M. Giovanni Grimani, a young nobleman, who, well aware that he had no right to command me, begged me in the most polite manner to call at his house to receive a letter which had been entrusted to him for delivery in my own hands. I went to him immediately, and after the usual compliments he handed me a letter with a flying seal, which he had received the day before.

Here are the contents:

"Sir, having made a useless search for my portrait after you left, and not being in the habit of receiving thieves in my apartment, I feel satisfied that it must be in your possession. I request you to deliver it to the person who will hand you this letter.

"Fogliazzi."

Happening to have the portrait with me, I took it out of my pocket, and gave it at once to M. Grimani, who received it with a mixture of satisfaction and surprise for he had evidently thought that the commission entrusted to him would be more difficult to fulfil, and he remarked,

"Love has most likely made a thief of you but I congratulate you, for your passion cannot be a very ardent one."

"How can you judge of that?"

"From the readiness with which you give up this portrait."

"I would not have given it up so easily to anybody else."

"I thank you; and as a compensation I beg you to accept my friendship."

"I place it in my estimation infinitely above the portrait, and even above the original. May I ask you to forward my answer?"

"I promise you to send it. Here is some paper, write your letter; you need not seal it."

I wrote the following words:

"In getting rid of the portrait, Casanova experiences a satisfaction by far superior to that which he felt when, owing to a stupid fancy, he was foolish enough to put it in his pocket."

Bad weather having compelled the authorities to postpone the wonderful wedding until the following Sunday, I accompanied M. de Bragadin, who was going to Padua. The amiable old man ran away from, the noisy pleasures which no longer suited his age, and he was going to spend in peace the few days which the public rejoicings would have rendered unpleasant for him in Venice. On the following Saturday, after dinner, I bade him farewell, and got into the post-chaise to return to Venice. If I had left Padua two minutes sooner or later, the whole course of my life would have been altered, and my destiny, if destiny is truly shaped by fatal combinations, would have been very different. But the reader can judge for himself.

Having, therefore, left Padua at the very instant marked by fatality, I met at Oriago a cabriolet, drawn at full speed by two post-horses, containing a very pretty woman and a man wearing a German uniform. Within a few yards from me the vehicle was suddenly upset on the side of the river, and the woman, falling over the officer, was in great danger of rolling into the Brenta. I jumped out of my chaise without even stopping my postillion, and rushing to the assistance of the lady I remedied with a chaste hand the disorder caused to her toilet by her fall.

Her companion, who had picked himself up without any injury, hastened towards us, and there was the lovely creature sitting on the ground thoroughly amazed, and less confused from her fall than from the indiscretion of her petticoats, which had exposed in all their nakedness certain parts which an honest woman never shews to a stranger. In the warmth of her thanks, which lasted until her postillion and mine had righted the cabriolet, she often called me her saviour, her guardian angel.

The vehicle being all right, the lady continued her journey towards Padua, and I resumed mine towards Venice, which I reached just in time to dress for the opera.

The next day I masked myself early to accompany the Bucentoro, which, favoured by fine weather, was to be taken to the Lido for the great and ridiculous ceremony. The whole affair is under the responsibility of the admiral of the arsenal, who answers for the weather remaining fine, under penalty of his head, for the slightest contrary wind might capsize the ship and drown the Doge, with all the most serene noblemen, the ambassadors, and the Pope's nuncio, who is the sponsor of that burlesque wedding which the Venetians respect even to superstition. To crown the misfortune of such an accident it would make the whole of Europe laugh, and people would not fail to say that the Doge of Venice had gone at last to consummate his marriage.

I had removed my mask, and was drinking some coffee under the 'procuraties' of St. Mark's Square, when a fine-looking female mask struck me gallantly on the shoulder with her fan. As I did not know who she was I did not take much notice of it, and after I had finished my coffee I put on my mask and walked towards the Spiaggia del Sepulcro, where M. de Bragadin's gondola was waiting for me. As I was getting near the Ponte del Paglia I saw the same masked woman attentively looking at some wonderful monster shewn for a few pence. I went up to her; and asked her why she had struck me with her fan.

"To punish you for not knowing me again after having saved my life." I guessed that she was the person I had rescued the day before on the banks of the Brenta, and after paying her some compliments I enquired whether she intended to follow the Bucentoro.

"I should like it," she said, "if I had a safe gondola."

I offered her mine, which was one of the largest, and, after consulting a masked person who accompanied her, she accepted. Before stepping in I invited them to take off their masks, but they told me that they wished to remain unknown. I then begged them to tell me if they belonged to the suite of some ambassador, because in that case I should be compelled, much to my regret, to withdraw my invitation; but they assured me that they were both Venetians. The gondola belonging to a patrician, I might have committed myself with the State Inquisitors-a thing which I wished particularly to avoid. We were following the Bucentoro, and seated near the lady I allowed myself a few slight liberties, but she foiled my intentions by changing her seat. After the ceremony we returned to Venice, and the officer who accompanied the lady told me that I would oblige them by dining in their company at "The Savage." I accepted, for I felt somewhat curious about the woman. What I had seen of her at the time of her fall warranted my curiosity. The officer left me alone with her, and went before us to order dinner.

As soon as I was alone with her, emboldened by the mask, I told her that I was in love with her, that I had a box at the opera, which I placed entirely at her disposal, and that, if she would only give me the hope that I was not wasting my time and my attentions, I would remain her humble servant during the carnival.

"If you mean to be cruel," I added, "pray say so candidly."

"I must ask you to tell me what sort of a woman you take me for?"

"For a very charming one, whether a princess or a maid of low degree. Therefore, I hope that you will give me, this very day, some marks of your kindness, or I must part with you immediately after dinner."

"You will do as you please; but I trust that after dinner you will have changed your opinion and your language, for your way of speaking is not pleasant. It seems to me that, before venturing upon such an explanation, it is necessary to know one another. Do you not think so?"

"Yes, I do; but I am afraid of being deceived."

"How very strange! And that fear makes you begin by what ought to be the end?"

"I only beg to-day for one encouraging word. Give it to me and I will at once be modest, obedient and discreet."

"Pray calm yourself."

We found the officer waiting for us before the door of "The Savage," and went upstairs. The moment we were in the room, she took off her mask, and I thought her more beautiful than the day before. I wanted only to ascertain, for the sake of form and etiquette, whether the officer was her husband, her lover, a relative or a protector, because, used as I was to gallant adventures, I wished to know the nature of the one in which I was embarking.

We sat down to dinner, and the manners of the gentleman and of the lady made it necessary for me to be careful. It was to him that I offered my box, and it was accepted; but as I had none, I went out after dinner under pretence of some engagement, in order to get one at the opera-buffa, where Petrici and Lasqui were then the shining stars. After the opera I gave them a good supper at an inn, and I took them to their house in my gondola. Thanks to the darkness of the night, I obtained from the pretty woman all the favours which can be granted by the side of a third person who has to be treated with caution. As we parted company, the officer said,

"You shall hear from me to-morrow."

"Where, and how?"

"Never mind that."

The next morning the servant announced an officer; it was my man. After we had exchanged the usual compliments, after I had thanked him for the honour he had done me the day before, I asked him to tell me his name. He answered me in the following manner, speaking with great fluency, but without looking at me:

"My name is P— C—. My father is rich, and enjoys great consideration at the exchange; but we are not on friendly terms at present. I reside in St. Mark's Square. The lady you saw with me was a Mdlle. O—; she is the wife of the broker C—, and her sister married the patrician P— M—. But Madame C— is at variance with her husband on my account, as she is the cause of my quarrel with my father.

"I wear this uniform in virtue of a captaincy in the Austrian service, but I have never served in reality. I have the contract for the supply of oxen to the City of Venice, and I get the cattle from Styria and Hungary. This contract gives me a net profit of ten thousand florins a year; but an unforeseen embarrassment, which I must remedy; a fraudulent bankruptcy, and some extraordinary expenditure, place me for the present in monetary difficulties. Four years ago I heard a great deal about you, and wished very much to make your acquaintance; I firmly believe that it was through the interference of Heaven that we became acquainted the day before yesterday. I have no hesitation in claiming from you an important service which will unite us by the ties of the warmest friendship. Come to my assistance without running any risk yourself; back these three bills of exchange. You need not be afraid of having to pay them, for I will leave in your hands these three other bills which fall due before the first. Besides, I will give you a mortgage upon the proceeds of my contract during the whole year, so that, should I fail to take up these bills, you could seize my cattle in Trieste, which is the only road through which they can come."

Astonished at his speech and at his proposal, which seemed to me a lure and made me fear a world of trouble which I always abhorred, struck by the strange idea of that man who, thinking that I would easily fall into the snare, gave me the preference over so many other persons whom he certainly knew better than me, I did not hesitate to tell him that I would never accept his offer. He then had recourse to all his eloquence to persuade me, but I embarrassed him greatly by telling him how surprised I was at his giving me the preference over all his other acquaintances, when I had had the honour to know him only for two days.

"Sir" he said, with barefaced impudence, "having recognised in you a man of great intelligence, I felt certain that you would at once see the advantages of my offer, and that you would not raise any objection."

"You must see your mistake by this time, and most likely you will take me for a fool now you see that I should believe myself a dupe if I accepted."

He left me with an apology for having troubled me, and saying that he hoped to see me in the evening at St. Mark's Square, where he would be with Madame C—, he gave me his address, telling me that he had retained possession of his apartment unknown to his father. This was as much as to say that he expected me to return his visit, but if I had been prudent I should not have done so.

Disgusted at the manner in which that man had attempted to get hold of me, I no longer felt any inclination to try my fortune with his mistress, for it seemed evident that they were conspiring together to make a dupe of me, and as I had no wish to afford them that gratification I avoided them in the evening. It would have been wise to keep to that line of conduct; but the next day, obeying my evil genius, and thinking that a polite call could not have any consequences, I called upon him.

A servant having taken me to his room, he gave me the most friendly welcome, and reproached me in a friendly manner for not having shewn myself the evening before. After that, he spoke again of his affairs, and made me look at a heap of papers and documents; I found it very wearisome.

"If you make up your mind to sign the three bills of exchange," he said, "I will take you as a partner in my contract."

By this extraordinary mark of friendship, he was offering me—at least he said so—an income of five thousand florins a year; but my only answer was to beg that the matter should never be mentioned again. I was going to take leave of him, when he said that he wished to introduce me to his mother and sister.

He left the room, and came back with them. The mother was a respectable, simple-looking woman, but the daughter was a perfect beauty; she literally dazzled me. After a few minutes, the over-trustful mother begged leave to retire, and her daughter remained. In less than half an hour I was captivated; her perfection delighted me; her lively wit, her artless reasoning, her candour, her ingenuousness, her natural and noble feelings, her cheerful and innocent quickness, that harmony which arises from beauty, wit, and innocence, and which had always the most powerful influence over me—everything in fact conspired to make me the slave of the most perfect woman that the wildest dreams could imagine.

Mdlle. C— C— never went out without her mother who, although very pious, was full of kind indulgence. She read no books but her father's—a serious man who had no novels in his library, and she was longing to read some tales of romance. She had likewise a great wish to know Venice, and as no one visited the family she had never been told that she was truly a prodigy of beauty. Her brother was writing while I conversed with her, or rather answered all the questions which she addressed to me, and which I could only satisfy by developing the ideas that she already had, and that she was herself amazed to find in her own mind, for her soul had until then been unconscious of its own powers. Yet I did not tell her that she was lovely and that she interested me in the highest degree, because I had so often said the same to other women, and without truth, that I was afraid of raising her suspicions.

I left the house with a sensation of dreamy sadness; feeling deeply moved by the rare qualities I had discovered in that charming girl, I promised myself not to see her again, for I hardly thought myself the man to sacrifice my liberty entirely and to ask her in marriage, although I certainly believed her endowed with all the qualities necessary to minister to my happiness.

I had not seen Madame Manzoni since my return to Venice, and I went to pay her a visit. I found the worthy woman the same as she had always been towards me, and she gave me the most affectionate welcome. She told me that Therese Imer, that pretty girl who had caused M. de Malipiero to strike me thirteen years before, had just returned from Bayreuth, where the margrave had made her fortune. As she lived in the house opposite, Madame Manzoni, who wanted to enjoy her surprise, sent her word to come over. She came almost immediately, holding by the hand a little boy of eight years—a lovely child—and the only one she had given to her husband, who was a dancer in Bayreuth. Our surprise at seeing one another again was equal to the pleasure we experienced in recollecting what had occurred in our young days; it is true that we had but trifles to recollect. I congratulated her upon her good fortune, and judging of my position from external appearances, she thought it right to congratulate me, but her fortune would have been established on a firmer basis than mine if she had followed a prudent line of conduct. She unfortunately indulged in numerous caprices with which my readers will become acquainted. She was an excellent musician, but her fortune was not altogether owing to her talent; her charms had done more for her than anything else. She told me her adventures, very likely with some restrictions, and we parted after a conversation of two hours. She invited me to breakfast for the following day. She told me that the margrave had her narrowly watched, but being an old acquaintance I was not likely to give rise to any suspicion; that is the aphorism of all women addicted to gallantry. She added that I could, if I liked, see her that same evening in her box, and that M. Papafava, who was her god-father, would be glad to see me. I called at her house early the next morning, and I found her in bed with her son, who, thanks to the principles in which he had been educated, got up and left the room as soon as he saw me seated near his mother's bed. I spent three hours with her, and I recollect that the last was delightful; the reader will know the consequence of that pleasant hour later. I saw her a second time during the fortnight she passed in Venice, and when she left I promised to pay her a visit in Bayreuth, but I never kept my promise.

I had at that time to attend to the affairs of my posthumous brother, who had, as he said, a call from Heaven to the priesthood, but he wanted a patrimony. Although he was ignorant and devoid of any merit save a handsome face, he thought that an ecclesiastical career would insure his happiness, and he depended a great deal upon his preaching, for which, according to the opinion of the women with whom he was acquainted, he had a decided talent. I took everything into my hands, and I succeeded in obtaining for him a patrimony from M. Grimani, who still owed us the value of the furniture in my father's house, of which he had never rendered any account. He transferred to him a life-interest in a house in Venice, and two years afterwards my brother was ordained. But the patrimony was only fictitious, the house being already mortgaged; the Abbe Grimani was, however, a kind Jesuit, and those sainted servants of God think that all is well that ends well and profitably to themselves. I shall speak again of my unhappy brother whose destiny became involved with mine.

Two days had passed since I had paid my visit to P— C—, when I met him in the street. He told me that his sister was constantly speaking of me, that she quoted a great many things which I had told her, and that his mother was much pleased at her daughter having made my acquaintance. "She would be a good match for you," he added, "for she will have a dowry of ten thousand ducats. If you will call on me to-morrow, we will take coffee with my mother and sister."

I had promised myself never again to enter his house, but I broke my word. It is easy enough for a man to forget his promises under such circumstances.

I spent three hours in conversation with the charming girl and when I left her I was deeply in love. As I went away, I told her that I envied the destiny of the man who would have her for his wife, and my compliment, the first she had ever received, made her blush.

After I had left her I began to examine the nature of my feelings towards her, and they frightened me, for I could neither behave towards Mdlle. C— C— as an honest man nor as a libertine. I could not hope to obtain her hand, and I almost fancied I would stab anyone who advised me to seduce her. I felt that I wanted some diversion: I went to the gaming-table. Playing is sometimes an excellent lenitive to calm the mind, and to smother the ardent fire of love. I played with wonderful luck, and I was going home with plenty of gold, when in a solitary narrow street I met a man bent down less by age than by the heavy weight of misery. As I came near him I recognized Count Bonafede, the sight of whom moved me with pity. He recognized me likewise. We talked for some time, and at last he told me the state of abject poverty to which he was reduced, and the great difficulty he had to keep his numerous family. "I do not blush," he added, "in begging from you one sequin which will keep us alive for five or six days." I immediately gave him ten, trying to prevent him from lowering himself in his anxiety to express his gratitude, but I could not prevent him from shedding tears.

As we parted, he told me that what made him most miserable was to see the position of his daughter, who had become a great beauty, and would rather die than make a sacrifice of her virtue. "I can neither support her in those feelings," he said, with a sigh, "nor reward her for them."

Thinking that I understood the wishes with which misery had inspired him, I took his address, and promised to pay him a visit. I was curious to see what had become of a virtue of which I did not entertain a very high opinion. I called the next day. I found a house almost bare of furniture, and the daughter alone—a circumstance which did not astonish me. The young countess had seen me arrive, and received me on the stairs in the most amiable manner. She was pretty well dressed, and I thought her handsome, agreeable, and lively, as she had been when I made her acquaintance in Fort St. Andre. Her father having announced my visit, she was in high spirits, and she kissed me with as much tenderness as if I had been a beloved lover. She took me to her own room, and after she had informed me that her mother was ill in bed and unable to see me, she gave way again to the transport of joy which, as she said, she felt in seeing me again. The ardour of our mutual kisses, given at first under the auspices of friendship, was not long in exciting our senses to such an extent that in less than a quarter of an hour I had nothing more to desire. When it was all over, it became us both, of course, to be, or at least to appear to be, surprised at what had taken place, and I could not honestly hesitate to assure the poor countess that it was only the first token of a constant and true love. She believed it, or she feigned to believe it, and perhaps I myself fancied it was true—for the moment. When we had become calm again, she told me the fearful state to which they were reduced, her brothers walking barefooted in the streets, and her father having positively no bread to give them.

"Then you have not any lover?"

"What? a lover! Where could I find a man courageous enough to be my lover in such a house as this? Am I a woman to sell myself to the first comer for the sum of thirty sous? There is not a man in Venice who would think me worth more than that, seeing me in such a place as this. Besides, I was not born for prostitution."

Such a conversation was not very cheerful; she was weeping, and the spectacle of her sadness, joined to the picture of misery which surrounded me, was not at all the thing to excite love. I left her with a promise to call again, and I put twelve sequins in her hand. She was surprised at the amount; she had never known herself so rich before. I have always regretted I did not give her twice as much.

The next day P— C— called on me, and said cheerfully that his mother had given permission to her daughter to go to the opera with him, that the young girl was delighted because she had never been there before, and that, if I liked, I could wait for them at some place where they would meet me.

"But does your sister know that you intend me to join you?"

"She considers it a great pleasure."

"Does your mother know it?"

"No; but when she knows it she will not be angry, for she has a great esteem for you."

"In that case I will try to find a private box."

"Very well; wait for us at such a place."

The scoundrel did not speak of his letters of exchange again, and as he saw that I was no longer paying my attentions to his mistress, and that I was in love with his sister, he had formed the fine project of selling her to me. I pitied the mother and the daughter who had confidence in such a man; but I had not the courage to resist the temptation. I even went so far as to persuade myself that as I loved her it was my duty to accept the offer, in order to save her from other snares; for if I had declined her brother might have found some other man less scrupulous, and I could not bear the idea. I thought that in my company her innocence ran no risk.

I took a box at the St. Samuel Opera, and I was waiting for them at the appointed place long before the time. They came at last, and the sight of my young friend delighted me. She was elegantly masked, and her brother wore his uniform. In order not to expose the lovely girl to being recognized on account of her brother, I made them get into my gondola. He insisted upon being landed near the house of his mistress, who was ill, he said, and he added that he would soon join us in our box. I was astonished that C— C— did not shew any surprise or repugnance at remaining alone with me in the gondola; but I did not think the conduct of her brother extraordinary, for it was evident that it was all arranged beforehand in his mind.

I told C— C— that we would remain in the gondola until the opening of the theatre, and that as the heat was intense she would do well to take off her mask, which she did at once. The law I had laid upon myself to respect her, the noble confidence which was beaming on her countenance and in her looks, her innocent joy—everything increased the ardour of my love.

Not knowing what to say to her, for I could speak to her of nothing but love—and it was a delicate subject—I kept looking at her charming face, not daring to let my eyes rest upon two budding globes shaped by the Graces, for fear of giving the alarm to her modesty. "Speak to me," she said at last; "you only look at me without uttering a single word. You have sacrificed yourself for me, because my brother would have taken you with him to his lady-love, who, to judge from what he says, must be as beautiful as an angel."

"I have seen that lady."

"I suppose she is very witty."

"She may be so; but I have no opportunity of knowing, for I have never visited her, and I do not intend ever to call upon her. Do not therefore imagine, beautiful C— C—, that I have made the slightest sacrifice for your sake."

"I was afraid you had, because as you did not speak I thought you were sad."

"If I do not speak to you it is because I am too deeply moved by your angelic confidence in me."

"I am very glad it is so; but how could I not trust you? I feel much more free, much more confident with you than with my brother himself. My mother says it is impossible to be mistaken, and that you are certainly an honest man. Besides, you are not married; that is the first thing I asked my brother. Do you recollect telling me that you envied the fate of the man who would have me for his wife? Well, at that very moment I was thinking that your wife would be the happiest woman in Venice."

These words, uttered with the most candid artlessness, and with that tone of sincerity which comes from the heart, had upon me an effect which it would be difficult to describe; I suffered because I could not imprint the most loving kiss upon the sweet lips which had just pronounced them, but at the same time it caused me the most delicious felicity to see that such an angel loved me.

"With such conformity of feelings," I said, "we would, lovely C—, be perfectly happy, if we could be united for ever. But I am old enough to be your father."

"You my father? You are joking! Do you know that I am fourteen?"

"Do you know that I am twenty-eight?"

　　　　　　　　　　　　　　　　GIACOMO CASANOVA

"Well, where can you see a man of your age having a daughter of mine? If my father were like you, he would certainly never frighten me; I could not keep anything from him."

The hour to go to the theatre had come; we landed, and the performance engrossed all her attention. Her brother joined us only when it was nearly over; it had certainly been a part of his calculation. I took them to an inn for supper, and the pleasure I experienced in seeing the charming girl eat with a good appetite made me forget that I had had no dinner. I hardly spoke during the supper, for love made me sick, and I was in a state of excitement which could not last long. In order to excuse my silence, I feigned to be suffering from the toothache.

After supper, P— C— told his sister that I was in love with her, and that I should certainly feel better if she would allow me to kiss her. The only answer of the innocent girl was to offer me her laughing lips, which seemed to call for kisses. I was burning; but my respect for that innocent and naive young creature was such that I only kissed her cheek, and even that in a manner very cold in appearance.

"What a kiss!" exclaimed P— C—. "Come, come, a good lover's kiss!"

I did not move; the impudent fellow annoyed me; but his sister, turning her head aside sadly, said,

"Do not press him; I am not so happy as to please him."

That remark gave the alarm to my love; I could no longer master my feelings.

"What!" I exclaimed warmly, "what! beautiful C—, you do not condescend to ascribe my reserve to the feeling which you have inspired me with? You suppose that you do not please me? If a kiss is all that is needed to prove the contrary to you, oh! receive it now with all the sentiment that is burning in my heart!"

Then folding her in my arms, and pressing her lovingly against my breast, I imprinted on her mouth the long and ardent kiss which I had so much wished to give her; but the nature of that kiss made the timid dove feel that she had fallen into the vulture's claws. She escaped from my arms, amazed at having discovered my love in such a manner. Her brother expressed his approval, while she replaced her mask over her face, in order to conceal her confusion. I asked her whether she had any longer any doubts as to my love.

"You have convinced me," she answered, "but, because you have undeceived me, you must not punish me."

I thought that this was a very delicate answer, dictated by true sentiment; but her brother was not pleased with it, and said it was foolish.

We put on our masks, left the inn, and after I had escorted them to their house I went home deeply in love, happy in my inmost soul, yet very sad.

The reader will learn in the following chapters the progress of my love and the adventures in which I found myself engaged.

III

Progress of My Intrigue with the Beautiful C. C.

The next morning P— C— called on me with an air of triumph; he told me that his sister had confessed to her mother that we loved one another, and that if she was ever to be married she would be unhappy with any other husband.

"I adore your sister," I said to him; "but do you think that your father will be willing to give her to me?"

"I think not; but he is old. In the mean time, love one another. My mother has given her permission to go to the opera this evening with us."

"Very well, my dear friend, we must go."

"I find myself under the necessity of claiming a slight service at your hands."

"Dispose of me."

"There is some excellent Cyprus wine to be sold very cheap, and I can obtain a cask of it against my bill at six months. I am certain of selling it again immediately with a good profit; but the merchant requires a guarantee, and he is disposed to accept yours, if you will give it. Will you be kind enough to endorse my note of hand?"

"With pleasure."

I signed my name without hesitation, for where is the man in love who in such a case would have refused that service to a person who to revenge himself might have made him miserable? We made an appointment for the evening, and parted highly pleased with each other.

After I had dressed myself, I went out and bought a dozen pairs of gloves, as many pairs of silk stockings, and a pair of garters embroidered in gold and with gold clasps, promising myself much pleasure in offering that first present to my young friend.

I need not say that I was exact in reaching the appointed place, but they were there already, waiting for me. Had I not suspected the intentions of P— C—, their coming so early would have been very flattering to my vanity. The moment I had joined them, P— C— told me that, having other engagements to fulfil, he would leave his sister with me, and meet us at the theatre in the evening. When he had gone,

I told C— C— that we would sail in a gondola until the opening of the theatre.

"No," she answered, "let us rather go to the Zuecca Garden."

"With all my heart."

I hired a gondola and we went to St. Blaze, where I knew a very pretty garden which, for one sequin, was placed at my disposal for the remainder of the day, with the express condition that no one else would be allowed admittance. We had not had any dinner, and after I had ordered a good meal we went up to a room where we took off our disguises and masks, after which we went to the garden.

My lovely C— C— had nothing on but a bodice made of light silk and a skirt of same description, but she was charming in that simple costume! My amorous looks went through those light veils, and in my imagination I saw her entirely naked! I sighed with burning desires, with a mixture of discreet reserve and voluptuous love.

The moment we had reached the long avenue, my young companion, as lively as a fawn, finding herself at liberty on the green sward, and enjoying that happy freedom for the first time in her life, began to run about and to give way to the spirit of cheerfulness which was natural to her. When she was compelled to stop for want of breath, she burst out laughing at seeing me gazing at her in a sort of ecstatic silence. She then challenged me to run a race; the game was very agreeable to me. I accepted, but I proposed to make it interesting by a wager.

"Whoever loses the race," I said, "shall have to do whatever the winner asks."

"Agreed!"

We marked the winning-post, and made a fair start. I was certain to win, but I lost on purpose, so as to see what she would ask me to do. At first she ran with all her might while I reserved my strength, and she was the first to reach the goal. As she was trying to recover her breath, she thought of sentencing me to a good penance: she hid herself behind a tree and told me, a minute afterwards, that I had to find her ring. She had concealed it about her, and that was putting me in possession of all her person. I thought it was a delightful forfeit, for I could easily see that she had chosen it with intentional mischief; but I felt that I ought not to take too much advantage of her, because her artless confidence required to be encouraged. We sat on the grass, I visited her pockets, the folds of her stays, of her petticoat; then I looked in her shoes, and even at her garters which were fastened below the knees. Not finding anything, I kept on my search, and as the ring was about her, I was of course bound to discover it. My reader has most likely guessed that I had some suspicion of the charming hiding-place in which the young beauty had concealed the ring, but before coming to it I wanted to enjoy myself. The ring was at last found between the two most beautiful keepers that nature had ever rounded, but I felt such emotion as I drew it out that my hand was trembling.

"What are you trembling for?" she asked.

"Only for joy at having found the ring; you had concealed it so well! But you owe me a revenge, and this time you shall not beat me."

"We shall see."

We began a new race, and seeing that she was not running very fast, I thought I could easily distance her whenever I liked. I was mistaken. She had husbanded her strength, and when we had run about two-thirds of the race she suddenly sprang forward at full speed, left me behind, and I saw that I had lost. I then thought of a trick, the effect of which never fails; I feigned a heavy fall, and I uttered a shriek of pain. The poor child stopped at once, ran back to me in great fright, and, pitying me, she assisted me to raise myself from the ground. The moment I was on my feet again, I laughed heartily and, taking a spring forward, I had reached the goal long before her.

The charming runner, thoroughly amazed, said to me,

"Then you did not hurt yourself?"

"No, for I fell purposely."

"Purposely? Oh, to deceive me! I would never have believed you capable of that. It is not fair to win by fraud; therefore I have not lost the race."

"Oh! yes, you have, for I reached the goal before you."

"Trick for trick; confess that you tried to deceive me at the start."

"But that is fair, and your trick is a very different thing."

"Yet it has given me the victory, and

> "*Vincasi per fortund o per ingano,*
> *Il vincer sempre fu laudabil cosa*" . . .

"I have often heard those words from my brother, but never from my father. Well, never mind, I have lost. Give your judgment now, I will obey."

"Wait a little. Let me see. Ah! my sentence is that you shall exchange your garters for mine."

"Exchange our garters! But you have seen mine, they are ugly and worth nothing."

"Never mind. Twice every day I shall think of the person I love, and as nearly as possible at the same hours you will have to think of me."

"It is a very pretty idea, and I like it. Now I forgive you for having deceived me. Here are my ugly garters! Ah! my dear deceiver, how beautiful yours are! What a handsome present! How they will please my mother! They must be a present which you have just received, for they are quite new."

"No, they have not been given to me. I bought them for you, and I have been racking my brain to find how I could make you accept them. Love suggested to me the idea of making them the prize of the race. You may now imagine my sorrow when I saw that you would win. Vexation inspired me with a deceitful stratagem which arose from a feeling you had caused yourself, and which turned entirely to your honour, for you must admit that you would have shewn a very hard heart if you had not come to my assistance."

"And I feel certain that you would not have had recourse to that stratagem, if you could have guessed how deeply it would pain me."

"Do you then feel much interest in me?"

"I would do anything in the world to convince you of it. I like my pretty garters exceedingly; I will never have another pair, and I promise you that my brother shall not steal them from me."

"Can you suppose him capable of such an action?"

"Oh! certainly, especially if the fastenings are in gold."

"Yes, they are in gold; but let him believe that they are in gilt brass."

"Will you teach me how to fasten my beautiful garters?"

"Of course I will."

We went upstairs, and after our dinner which we both enjoyed with a good appetite, she became more lively and I more excited by love, but at the same time more to be pitied in consequence of the restraint to which I had condemned myself. Very anxious to try her garters, she begged me to help her, and that request was made in good faith, without mischievous coquetry. An innocent young girl, who, in spite of her fifteen years, has not loved yet, who has not frequented the society of other girls, does not know the violence of amorous desires or what is likely to excite them. She has no idea of the danger of a tete-a-tete.

When a natural instinct makes her love for the first time, she believes the object of her love worthy of her confidence, and she thinks that to be loved herself she must shew the most boundless trust.

Seeing that her stockings were too short to fasten the garter above the knee, she told me that she would in future use longer ones, and I immediately offered her those that I had purchased. Full of gratitude she sat on my knees, and in the effusion of her satisfaction she bestowed upon me all the kisses that she would have given to her father if he had made her such a present. I returned her kisses, forcibly keeping down the violence of my feelings. I only told her that one of her kisses was worth a kingdom. My charming C— C— took off her shoes and stockings, and put on one of the pairs I had given her, which went halfway up her thigh. The more innocent I found her to be, the less I could make up my mind to possess myself of that ravishing prey.

We returned to the garden, and after walking about until the evening we went to the opera, taking care to keep on our masks, because, the theatre being small, we might easily have been recognized, and my lovely friend was certain that her father would not allow her to come out again, if he found out that she had gone to the opera.

We were rather surprised not to see her brother. On our left we had the Marquis of Montalegre, the Spanish ambassador, with his acknowledged mistress, Mdlle. Bola, and in the box on our right a man and a woman who had not taken off their masks. Those two persons kept their eyes constantly fixed upon us, but my young friend did not remark it as her back was turned towards them. During the ballet, C— C— having left the libretto of the opera on the ledge of the box, the man with the mask stretched forth his hand and took it. That proved to me that we were known to him, and I said so to my companion, who turned round and recognized her brother. The lady who was with him could be no other than Madame C—. As P— C— knew the number of our box, he had taken the next one; he could not have done so without some intention, and I foresaw that he meant to make his sister have supper with that woman. I was much annoyed, but I could not prevent it without breaking off with him, altogether, and I was in love.

After the second ballet, he came into our box with his lady, and after the usual exchange of compliments the acquaintance was made, and we had to accept supper at his casino. As soon as the two ladies had thrown off their masks, they embraced one another, and the mistress of P— C— overwhelmed my young friend with compliments and attentions.

At table she affected to treat her with extreme affability, and C— C— not having any experience of the world behaved towards her with the greatest respect. I could, however, see that C—, in spite of all her art, could hardly hide the vexation she felt at the sight of the superior beauty which I had preferred to her own charms. P— C—, who was of an extravagant gaiety, launched forth in stupid jokes at which his mistress alone laughed; in my anger, I shrugged my shoulders, and his sister, not understanding his jests, took no notice of them. Altogether our 'partie caree' was not formed of congenial spirits, and was rather a dull affair.

As the dessert was placed on the table, P— C—, somewhat excited by the wine he had drunk, kissed his lady-love, and challenged me to follow his example with his sister. I told him that I loved Mdlle. C— C— truly, and that I would not take such liberties with her until I should have acquired a legal right to her favours. P— C— began to scoff at what I had said, but C— stopped him. Grateful for that mark of propriety, I took out of my pocket the twelve pairs of gloves which I had bought in the morning, and after I had begged her acceptance of half a dozen pairs I gave the other six to my young friend. P— C— rose from the table with a sneer, dragging along with him his mistress, who had likewise drunk rather freely, and he threw himself on a sofa with her. The scene taking a lewd turn, I placed myself in such a manner as to hide them from the view of my young friend, whom I led into the recess of a window. But I had not been able to prevent C— C— from seeing in a looking-glass the position of the two impudent wretches, and her face was suffused with blushes; I, however, spoke to her quietly of indifferent things, and recovering her composure she answered me, speaking of her gloves, which she was folding on the pier-table. After his brutal exploit, P— C— came impudently to me and embraced me; his dissolute companion, imitating his example, kissed my young friend, saying she was certain that she had seen nothing. C— C— answered modestly that she did not know what she could have seen, but the look she cast towards me made me understand all she felt. If the reader has any knowledge of the human heart, he must guess what my feelings were. How was it possible to endure such a scene going on in the presence of an innocent girl whom I adored, when I had to fight hard myself with my own burning desires so as not to abuse her innocence! I was on a bed of thorns! Anger and indignation, restrained by the reserve I was compelled to adopt for fear of losing the object of my ardent love, made me tremble all over. The inventors of hell would not have failed to place that suffering among its torments, if they had known it. The lustful P— C— had thought of giving me a great proof of his friendship by the disgusting action he had been guilty of, and he had reckoned as nothing the dishonour of his mistress, and the delicacy of his sister whom he had thus exposed to prostitution. I do not know how I contrived not to strangle him. The next day, when he called on me, I overwhelmed him with the most bitter reproaches, and he tried to excuse himself by saying that he never would have acted in that manner if he had not felt satisfied that I had already treated his sister in the tete-a-tete in the same way that he treated his mistress before us.

My love for C— C— became every instant more intense, and I had made up my mind to undertake everything necessary to save her from the fearful position in which her unworthy brother might throw her by selling her for his own profit to some man less scrupulous than I was. It seemed to me urgent. What a disgusting state of things! What an unheard-of species of seduction! What a strange way to gain my friendship! And I found myself under the dire necessity of dissembling with the man whom I despised most in the world! I had been told that he was deeply in debt, that he had been a bankrupt in Vienna, where he had a wife and a family of children, that in Venice he had compromised his father who had been obliged to turn him out of his house, and who, out of pity, pretended not to know that he had kept his room in it. He had seduced his wife, or rather his mistress, who had been driven away by her husband, and after he had squandered everything she possessed, and he found himself at the end of his wits, he had tried to turn her prostitution to advantage. His poor mother who idolized him had given him everything she had, even her own clothes, and I expected him to plague me again for some loan or security, but I was firmly resolved on refusing. I could not bear the idea of C— C— being the innocent cause of my ruin, and used as a tool by her brother to keep up his disgusting life.

Moved by an irresistible feeling, by what is called perfect love, I called upon P— C— on the following day, and, after I had told him that I adored his sister with the most honourable intentions, I tried to make him realize how deeply he had grieved me by forgetting all respect, and that modesty which the most inveterate libertine ought never to insult if he has any pretension to be worthy of respectable society.

"Even if I had to give up," I added, "the pleasure of seeing your angelic sister, I have taken the firm resolution of not keeping company with you; but I candidly warn you that I will do everything in my power to prevent her from going out with you, and from being the victim of some infamous bargain in your hands."

He excused himself again by saying that he had drunk too much, and that he did not believe that my love for his sister was such as to despise the gratification of my senses. He begged my pardon, he embraced me with tears in his eyes, and I would, perhaps have given way to my own emotion, when his mother and sister entered the room. They offered me their heart-felt thanks for the handsome present I had given to the young lady. I told the mother that I loved her daughter, and that my fondest hope was to obtain her for my wife.

"In the hope of securing that happiness, madam," I added, "I shall get a friend to speak to your husband as soon as I shall have secured a position giving me sufficient means to keep her comfortably, and to assure her happiness."

So saying I kissed her hand, and I felt so deeply moved that the tears ran down my cheeks. Those tears were sympathetic, and the excellent woman was soon crying like me. She thanked me affectionately, and left me with her daughter and her son, who looked as if he had been changed into a statue.

There are a great many mothers of that kind in the world, and very often they are women who have led a virtuous life; they do not suppose that deceit can exist, because their own nature understands only what is upright and true; but they are almost always the victims of their good faith, and of their trust in those who seem to them to be patterns of honesty. What I had told the mother surprised the daughter, but her astonishment was much greater when she heard of what I had said to her brother. After one moment of consideration, she told him that, with any other man but me, she would have been ruined; and that, if she had been in the place of Madame C—, she would never have forgiven him, because the way he had treated her was as debasing for her as for himself. P— C— was weeping, but the traitor could command tears whenever he pleased.

It was Whit Sunday, and as the theatres were closed he told me that, if I would be at the same place of Appointment as before, the next day, he would leave his sister with me, and go by himself with Madame C—, whom he could not honourably leave alone.

"I will give you my key," he added, "and you can bring back my sister here as soon as you have supper together wherever you like."

And he handed me his key, which I had not the courage to refuse. After that he left us. I went away myself a few minutes afterwards, having previously agreed with C— C— that we would go to the Zuecca Garden on the following day.

I was punctual, and love exciting me to the highest degree I foresaw what would happen on that day. I had engaged a box at the opera, and we went to our garden until the evening. As it was a holiday there were several small parties of friends sitting at various tables, and being unwilling to mix with other people we made up our minds to remain in the apartment which was given to us, and to go to the opera only towards the end of the performance. I therefore ordered a good supper. We had seven hours to spend together, and my charming young friend remarked that the time would certainly not seem long to us. She threw off her disguise and sat on my knees, telling me that I had completed the conquest of her heart by my reserve towards her during the supper with her brother; but all our conversation was accompanied by kisses which, little by little, were becoming more and more ardent.

"Did you see," she said to me, "what my brother did to Madame C— when she placed herself astride on his knees? I only saw it in the looking-glass, but I could guess what it was."

"Were you not afraid of my treating you in the same manner?"

"No, I can assure you. How could I possibly fear such a thing, knowing how much you love me? You would have humiliated me so deeply that I should no longer have loved you. We will wait until we are married, will we not, dear? You cannot realize the extent of the joy I felt when I heard you speak to my mother as you did! We will love each other for ever. But will you explain to me, dearest, the meaning of the words embroidered upon my garters?"

"Is there any motto upon them? I was not aware of it."

"Oh, yes! it is in French; pray read it."

Seated on my knees, she took off one of her garters while I was unclasping the other, and here are the two lines which I found embroidered on them, and which I ought to have read before offering them to her:

'En voyant chaque jour le bijou de ma belle,
Vous lui direz qu'Amour veut qu'il lui soit fidele.'

Those verses, rather free I must confess, struck me as very comic. I burst out laughing, and my mirth increased when, to please her, I had to translate their meaning. As it was an idea entirely new to her, I found it necessary to enter into particulars which lighted an ardent fire in our veins.

"Now," she observed, "I shall not dare to shew my garters to anybody, and I am very sorry for it."

As I was rather thoughtful, she added,

"Tell me what you are thinking of?"

"I am thinking that those lucky garters have a privilege which perhaps I shall never enjoy. How I wish myself in their place: I may die of that wish, and die miserable."

"No, dearest, for I am in the same position as you, and I am certain to live. Besides, we can hasten our marriage. As far as I am concerned, I am ready to become your wife to-morrow if you wish it. We are both free, and my father cannot refuse his consent."

"You are right, for he would be bound to consent for the sake of his honour. But I wish to give him a mark of my respect by asking for your hand, and after that everything will soon be ready. It might be in a week or ten days."

"So soon? You will see that my father will say that I am too young."

"Perhaps he is right."

"No; I am young, but not too young, and I am certain that I can be your wife."

I was on burning coals, and I felt that it was impossible for me to resist any longer the ardent fire which was consuming me.

"Oh, my best beloved!" I exclaimed, "do you feel certain of my love? Do you think me capable of deceiving you? Are you sure that you will never repent being my wife?"

"More than certain, darling; for you could not wish to make me unhappy."

"Well, then, let our marriage take place now. Let God alone receive our mutual pledges; we cannot have a better witness, for He knows the purity of our intentions. Let us mutually engage our faith, let us unite our destinies and be happy. We will afterwards legalize our tender love with your father's consent and with the ceremonies of the Church; in the mean time be mine, entirely mine."

"Dispose of me, dearest. I promise to God, I promise to you that, from this very moment and for ever, I will be your faithful wife; I will say the same to my father, to the priest who will bless our union—in fact, to everybody."

"I take the same oath towards you, darling, and I can assure you that we are now truly married. Come to my arms! Oh, dearest, complete my felicity!"

"Oh, dear! am I indeed so near happiness!"

After kissing her tenderly, I went down to tell the mistress of the house not to disturb us, and not to bring up our dinner until we called for it. During my short absence, my charming C— C— had thrown herself dressed on the bed, but I told her that the god of love disapproved of unnecessary veils, and in less than a minute I made of her a new Eve, beautiful in her nakedness as if she had just come out of the hands of the Supreme Artist. Her skin, as soft as satin, was dazzlingly white, and seemed still more so beside her splendid black hair which I had spread over her alabaster shoulders. Her slender figure, her prominent hips, her beautifully-modelled bosom, her large eyes, from which flashed the sparkle of amorous desire, everything about her was strikingly beautiful, and presented to my hungry looks the perfection of the mother of love, adorned by all the charms which modesty throws over the attractions of a lovely woman.

Beside myself, I almost feared lest my felicity should not prove real, or lest it should not be made perfect by complete enjoyment, when mischievous love contrived, in so serious a moment, to supply me with a reason for mirth.

"Is there by any chance a law to prevent the husband from undressing himself?" enquired beautiful C— C—.

"No, darling angel, no; and even if there were such a barbarous law, I would not submit to it."

In one instant, I had thrown off all my garments, and my mistress, in her turn, gave herself up to all the impulse of natural instinct and curiosity, for every part of my body was an entirely new thing to her. At last, as if she had had enough of the pleasure her eyes were enjoying, she pressed me against her bosom, and exclaimed,

"Oh! dearest, what a difference between you and my pillow!"

"Your pillow, darling? You are laughing; what do you mean?"

"Oh! it is nothing but a childish fancy; I am afraid you will be angry."

"Angry! How could I be angry with you, my love, in the happiest moment of my life?"

"Well, for several days past, I could not go to sleep without holding my pillow in my arms; I caressed it, I called it my dear husband; I fancied it was you, and when a delightful enjoyment had left me without movement, I would go to sleep, and in the morning find my pillow still between my arms."

My dear C— C— became my wife with the courage of a true heroine, for her intense love caused her to delight even in bodily pain. After three hours spent in delicious enjoyment, I got up and called for our supper. The repast was simple, but very good. We looked at one another without speaking, for how could we find words to express our feelings? We thought that our felicity was extreme, and we enjoyed it with the certainty that we could renew it at will.

The hostess came up to enquire whether we wanted anything, and she asked if we were not going to the opera, which everybody said was so beautiful.

"Have you never been to the opera?"

"Never, because it is too dear for people in our position. My daughter has such a wish to go, that, God forgive me for saying it! she would give herself, I truly believe, to the man who would take her there once."

"That would be paying very dear for it," said my little wife, laughing. "Dearest, we could make her happy at less cost, for that hurts very much."

"I was thinking of it, my love. Here is the key of the box, you can make them a present of it."

"Here is the key of a box at the St. Moses Theatre," she said to the hostess; "it costs two sequins; go instead of us, and tell your daughter to keep her rose-bud for something better."

"To enable you to amuse yourself, my good woman; take these two sequins," I added. "Let your daughter enjoy herself well."

The good hostess, thoroughly amazed at the generosity of her guests, ran in a great hurry to her daughter, while we were delighted at having laid ourselves under the pleasant necessity of again going to bed. She came up with her daughter, a handsome, tempting blonde, who insisted upon kissing the hands of her benefactors.

"She is going this minute with her lover," said the mother. "He is waiting for her; but I will not let her go alone with him, for he is not to be trusted; I am going with them."

"That is right, my good woman; but when you come back this evening, let the gondola wait for us; it will take us to Venice."

"What! Do you mean to remain here until we return?"

"Yes, for this is our wedding-day."

"To-day? God bless you!"

She then went to the bed, to put it to rights, and seeing the marks of my wife's virginity she came to my dear C— C— and, in her joy, kissed her, and immediately began a sermon for the special benefit of her daughter, shewing her those marks which, in her opinion, did infinite honour to the young bride: respectable marks, she said, which in our days the god of Hymen sees but seldom on his altar.

The daughter, casting down her beautiful blue eyes, answered that the same would certainly be seen on her wedding-day.

"I am certain of it," said the mother, "for I never lose sight of thee. Go and get some water in this basin, and bring it here. This charming bride must be in need of it."

The girl obeyed. The two women having left us, we went to bed, and four hours of ecstatic delights passed off with wonderful rapidity. Our last engagement would have lasted longer, if my charming sweetheart had not taken a fancy to take my place and to reverse the position. Worn out with happiness and enjoyment, we were going to sleep, when the hostess came to tell us that the gondola was waiting for us. I immediately got up to open the door, in the hope that she would amuse us with her description of the opera; but she left that task to her daughter, who had come up with her, and she went down again to prepare some coffee for us. The young girl assisted my sweetheart to dress, but now and then she would wink at me in a manner which made me think that she had more experience than her mother imagined.

Nothing could be more indiscreet than the eyes of my beloved mistress; they wore the irrefutable marks of her first exploits. It is true that she had just been fighting a battle which had positively made her a different being to what she was before the engagement.

We took some hot coffee, and I told our hostess to get us a nice dinner for the next day; we then left in the gondola. The dawn of day was breaking when we landed at St. Sophia's Square, in order to set the curiosity of the gondoliers at fault, and we parted happy, delighted, and certain that we were thoroughly married. I went to bed, having made up my mind to compel M. de Bragadin, through the power of the oracle, to obtain legally for me the hand of my beloved C— C—. I remained in bed until noon, and spent the rest of the day in playing with ill luck, as if Dame Fortune had wished to warn me that she did not approve of my love.

IV

CONTINUATION OF MY INTRIGUES WITH C. C.—M. DE BRAGADIN
ASKS THE HAND OF THAT YOUNG PERSON FOR ME—HER FATHER
REFUSES, AND SENDS HER TO A CONVENT—DE LA HAYE—I LOSE
ALL MY MONEY AT THE FASO-TABLE—MY PARTNERSHIP WITH
CROCE REPLENISHES MY PURSE—VARIOUS INCIDENTS

The happiness derived from my love had prevented me from attaching any importance to my losses, and being entirely engrossed with the thought of my sweetheart my mind did not seem to care for whatever did not relate to her.

I was thinking of her the next morning when her brother called on me with a beaming countenance, and said,

"I am certain that you have slept with my sister, and I am very glad of it. She does not confess as much, but her confession is not necessary. I will bring her to you to-day."

"You will oblige me, for I adore her, and I will get a friend of mine to ask her in marriage from your father in such a manner that he will not be able to refuse."

"I wish it may be so, but I doubt it. In the mean time, I find myself compelled to beg another service from your kindness. I can obtain, against a note of hand payable in six months, a ring of the value of two hundred sequins, and I am certain to sell it again this very day for the same amount. That sum, is very necessary to me just now, but the jeweller, who knows you, will not let me have it without your security. Will you oblige me in this instance? I know that you lost a great deal last night; if you want some money I will give you one hundred sequins, which you will return when the note of hand falls due."

How could I refuse him? I knew very well that I would be duped, but I loved his sister so much:

"I am ready," said I to him, "to sign the note of hand, but you are wrong in abusing my love for your sister in such a manner."

We went out, and the jeweller having accepted my security the bargain was completed. The merchant, who knew me only by name, thinking of paying me a great compliment, told P— C— that with my guarantee all his goods were at his service. I did not feel flattered by the compliment, but I thought I could see in it the knavery of P— C—, who was clever enough to find out, out of a hundred, the fool who without any reason placed confidence in me when I possessed nothing. It was thus that my angelic C— C—, who seemed made to insure my happiness, was the innocent cause of my ruin.

At noon P— C— brought his sister; and wishing most likely to prove its honesty—for a cheat always tries hard to do that—he gave me back the letter of exchange which I had endorsed for the Cyprus wine, assuring me likewise that at our next meeting he would hand me the one hundred sequins which he had promised me.

I took my mistress as usual to Zuecca; I agreed for the garden to be kept closed, and we dined under a vine-arbour. My dear C— C— seemed to me more beautiful since she was mine, and, friendship being united to love we felt a delightful sensation of happiness which shone on our features. The hostess, who had found me generous, gave us some excellent game and some very fine fish; her daughter served us. She also came to undress my little wife as soon as we had gone upstairs to give ourselves up to the sweet pleasures natural to a young married couple.

When we were alone my loved asked me what was the meaning of the one hundred sequins which her brother had promised to bring me, and I told her all that had taken place between him and me.

"I entreat you, darling," she said to me, "to refuse all the demands of my brother in future; he is, unfortunately, in such difficulties that he would at the end drag you down to the abyss into which he must fall."

This time our enjoyment seemed to us more substantial; we relished it with a more refined delight, and, so to speak, we reasoned over it.

"Oh, my best beloved!" she said to me, "do all in your power to render me pregnant; for in that case my father could no longer refuse his consent to my marriage, under the pretext of my being too young."

It was with great difficulty that I made her understand that the fulfilment of that wish, however much I shared it myself, was not entirely in our power; but that, under the circumstances, it would most probably be fulfilled sooner or later.

After working with all our might at the completion of that great undertaking, we gave several hours to a profound and delightful repose. As soon as we were awake I called for candles and coffee, and we set to work again in the hope of obtaining the mutual harmony of ecstatic enjoyment which was necessary to insure our future happiness. It was in the midst of our loving sport that the too early dawn surprised us, and we hurried back to Venice to avoid inquisitive eyes.

We renewed our pleasures on the Friday, but, whatever delight I may feel now in the remembrance of those happy moments, I will spare my readers the description of my new enjoyment, because they might not feel interested in such repetitions. I must therefore only say that, before parting on that day, we fixed for the following Monday, the last day of the carnival, our last meeting in the Garden of Zuecca. Death alone could have hindered me from keeping that appointment, for it was to be the last opportunity of enjoying our amorous sport.

On the Monday morning I saw P— C—, who confirmed the appointment for the same hour, and at the place previously agreed upon, and I was there in good time. In spite of the impatience of a lover, the first hour of expectation passes rapidly, but the second is mortally long. Yet the third and the fourth passed without my seeing my beloved mistress. I was in a state of fearful anxiety; I imagined the most terrible disasters. It seemed to me that if C— C— had been unable to go out her brother ought to have come to let me know it.

But some unexpected mishap might have detained him, and I could not go and fetch her myself at her house, even if I had feared nothing else than to miss them on the road. At last, as the church bells were tolling the Angelus, C— C— came alone, and masked.

"I was certain," she said, "that you were here, and here I am in spite of all my mother could say. You must be starving. My brother has not put in an appearance through the whole of this day. Let us go quickly to our garden, for I am very hungry too, and love will console us for all we have suffered today."

She had spoken very rapidly, and without giving me time to utter a single word; I had nothing more to ask her. We went off, and took a gondola to our garden. The wind was very high, it blew almost a hurricane, and the gondola having only one rower the danger was great. C— C—, who had no idea of it, was playing with me to make up for the restraint under which she had been all day; but her movements exposed the gondolier to danger; if he had fallen into the water, nothing could have saved us, and we would have found death on our way to pleasure. I told her to keep quiet, but, being anxious not to frighten her, I dared not acquaint her with the danger we were running. The gondolier, however, had not the same reasons for sparing her feelings, and he called out to us in a stentorian voice that, if we did not keep quiet, we were all lost. His threat had the desired effect, and we reached the landing without mishap. I paid the man generously, and he laughed for joy when he saw the money for which he was indebted to the bad weather.

We spent six delightful hours in our casino; this time sleep was not allowed to visit us. The only thought which threw a cloud over our felicity was that, the carnival being over, we did not know how to contrive our future meetings. We agreed, however, that on the following Wednesday morning I should pay a visit to her brother, and that she would come to his room as usual.

We took leave of our worthy hostess, who, entertaining no hope of seeing us again, expressed her sorrow and overwhelmed us with blessings. I escorted my darling, without any accident, as far as the door of her house, and went home.

I had just risen at noon, when to my great surprise I had a visit from De la Haye with his pupil Calvi, a handsome young man, but the very copy of his master in everything. He walked, spoke, laughed exactly like him; it was the same language as that of the Jesuits correct but rather harsh French. I thought that excess of imitation perfectly scandalous, and I could not help telling De la Haye that he ought to change his pupil's deportment, because such servile mimicry would only expose him to bitter raillery. As I was giving him my opinion on that subject, Bavois made his appearance, and when he had spent an hour in the company of the young man he was entirely of the same mind. Calvi died two or three years later. De la Haye, who was bent upon forming pupils, became, two or three months after Calvi's death, the tutor of the young Chevalier de Morosini, the nephew of the nobleman to whom Bavois was indebted for his rapid fortune, who was then the Commissioner of the Republic to settle its boundaries with the Austrian Government represented by Count Christiani.

I was in love beyond all measure, and I would not postpone an application on which my happiness depended any longer. After dinner, and as soon as everybody had retired, I begged M. de Bragadin and his two friends to grant me an audience of two hours in the room in which we were always inaccessible. There, without any preamble, I told them that I was in love with C— C—, and determined on carrying her off if they could not contrive to obtain her from her father for my wife. "The question at issue," I said to M. de Bragadin, "is how to give me a respectable position, and to guarantee a dowry of ten thousand ducats which the young lady would bring me." They answered that, if Paralis gave them the necessary instructions, they were ready to fulfil them.

That was all I wanted. I spent two hours in forming all the pyramids they wished, and the result was that M. de Bragadin himself would demand in my name the hand of the young lady; the oracle explaining the reason of that choice by stating that it must be the same person who would guarantee the dowry with his own fortune. The father of my mistress being then at his country-house, I told my friends that they would have due notice of his return, and that they were to be all three together when M. de Bragadin demanded the young lady's hand.

Well pleased with what I had done, I called on P— C— the next morning. An old woman, who opened the door for me, told me that he was not at home, but that his mother would see me. She came immediately with her daughter, and they both looked very sad, which at once struck me as a bad sign. C— C— told me that her brother was in prison for debt, and that it would be difficult to get him out of it because his debts amounted to a very large sum. The mother, crying bitterly, told me how deeply grieved she was at not being able to support him in the prison, and she shewed me the letter he had written to her, in which he requested her to deliver an enclosure to his sister. I asked C— C— whether I could read it; she handed it to me, and I saw that he begged her to speak to me in his behalf. As I returned it to her, I told her to write to him that I was not in a position to do anything for him, but I entreated the mother to accept twenty-five sequins, which would enable her to assist him by sending him one or two at a time. She made up her mind to take them only when her daughter joined her entreaties to mine.

After this painful scene I gave them an account of what I had done in order to obtain the hand of my young sweetheart. Madame C-— thanked me, expressed her appreciation of my honourable conduct, but she told me not to entertain any hope, because her husband, who was very stubborn in his ideas, had decided that his daughter should marry a merchant, and not before the age of eighteen. He was expected home that very day. As I was taking leave of them, my mistress contrived to slip in my hand a letter in which she told me that I could safely make use of the key which I had in my possession, to enter the house at midnight, and that I would find her in her brother's room. This news made me very happy, for, notwithstanding all the doubts of her mother, I hoped for success in obtaining her hand.

When I returned home, I told M. de Bragadin of the expected arrival of the father of my charming C— C—, and the kind old man wrote to him immediately in my presence. He requested him to name at what time he might call on him on important business. I asked M. de Bragadin not to send his letter until the following day.

The reader can very well guess that C— C— had not to wait for me long after midnight. I gained admittance without any difficulty, and I found my darling, who received me with open arms.

"You have nothing to fear," she said to me; "my father has arrived in excellent health, and everyone in the house is fast asleep."

"Except Love," I answered, "which is now inviting us to enjoy ourselves. Love will protect us, dearest, and to-morrow your father will receive a letter from my worthy protector."

At those words C— C— shuddered. It was a presentiment of the future.

She said to me,

"My father thinks of me now as if I were nothing but a child; but his eyes are going to be opened respecting me; he will examine my conduct, and God knows what will happen! Now, we are happy, even more than we were during our visits to Zuecca, for we can see each other every night without restraint. But what will my father do when he hears that I have a lover?"

"What can he do? If he refuses me your hand, I will carry you off, and the patriarch would certainly marry us. We shall be one another's for life."

"It is my most ardent wish, and to realize it I am ready to do anything; but, dearest, I know my father."

We remained two hours together, thinking less of our pleasures than of our sorrow; I went away promising to see her again the next night. The whole of the morning passed off very heavily for me, and at noon M. de Bragadin informed me that he had sent his letter to the father, who had answered that he would call himself on the following day to ascertain M. de Bragadin's wishes. At midnight I saw my beloved mistress again, and I gave her an account of all that had transpired. C— C— told me that the message of the senator had greatly puzzled her father, because, as he had never had any intercourse with that nobleman, he could not imagine what he wanted with him. Uncertainty, a sort of anxious dread, and a confused hope, rendered our enjoyment much less lively during the two hours which we spent together. I had no doubt that M. Ch. C— the father of my young friend, would 'go home immediately after his interview with M. de Bragadin, that he would ask his daughter a great many questions, and I feared lest C— C—, in her trouble and confusion, should betray herself. She felt herself that it might be so, and I could see how painfully anxious she was. I was extremely uneasy myself, and I suffered much because, not knowing how her father would look at the matter, I could not give her any advice. As a matter of course, it was necessary for her to conceal certain circumstances which would have prejudiced his mind against us; yet it was urgent to tell him the truth and to shew herself entirely submissive to his will. I found myself placed in a strange position, and above all, I regretted having made the all-important application, precisely because it was certain to have too decisive a result. I longed to get out of the state of indecision in which I was, and I was surprised to see my young mistress less anxious than I was. We parted with heavy hearts, but with the hope that the next night would again bring us together, for the contrary did not seem to us possible.

The next day, after dinner, M. Ch. C— called upon M. de Bragadin, but I did not shew myself. He remained a couple of hours with my three friends, and as soon as he had gone I heard that his answer had been what the mother had told me, but with the addition of a circumstance most painful to me—namely, that his daughter would pass the four years which were to elapse, before she could think of marriage, in a convent. As a palliative to his refusal he had added, that, if by that time I had a well-established position in the world, he might consent to our wedding.

That answer struck me as most cruel, and in the despair in which it threw me I was not astonished when the same night I found the door by which I used to gain admittance to C— C— closed and locked inside.

I returned home more dead than alive, and lost twenty-four hours in that fearful perplexity in which a man is often thrown when he feels himself bound to take a decision without knowing what to decide. I thought of carrying her off, but a thousand difficulties combined to prevent the execution of that scheme, and her brother was in prison. I saw how difficult it would be to contrive a correspondence with my wife, for I considered C— C— as such, much more than if our marriage had received the sanction of the priest's blessing or of the notary's legal contract.

Tortured by a thousand distressing ideas, I made up my mind at last to pay a visit to Madame C—. A servant opened the door, and informed me that madame had gone to the country; she could not tell me when she was expected to return to Venice. This news was a terrible thunder-bolt to me; I remained as motionless as a statue; for now that I had lost that last resource I had no means of procuring the slightest information.

I tried to look calm in the presence of my three friends, but in reality I was in a state truly worthy of pity, and the reader will perhaps realize it if I tell him that in my despair I made up my mind to call on P— C— in his prison, in the hope that he might give me some information.

My visit proved useless; he knew nothing, and I did not enlighten his ignorance. He told me a great many lies which I pretended to accept as gospel, and giving him two sequins I went away, wishing him a prompt release.

I was racking my brain to contrive some way to know the position of my mistress—for I felt certain it was a fearful one—and believing her to be unhappy I reproached myself most bitterly as the cause of her misery. I had reached such a state of anxiety that I could neither eat nor sleep.

Two days after the refusal of the father, M. de Bragadin and his two friends went to Padua for a month. I had not had the heart to go with them, and I was alone in the house. I needed consolation and I went to the gaming-table, but I played without attention and lost a great deal. I had already sold whatever I possessed of any value, and I owed money everywhere. I could expect no assistance except from my three kind friends, but shame prevented me from confessing my position to them. I was in that disposition which leads easily to self-destruction, and I was thinking of it as I was shaving myself before a toilet-glass, when the servant brought to my room a woman who had a letter for me. The woman came up to me, and, handing me the letter, she said,

"Are you the person to whom it is addressed?"

I recognized at once a seal which I had given to C— C—; I thought I would drop down dead. In order to recover my composure, I told the woman to wait, and tried to shave myself, but my hand refused to perform its office. I put the razor down, turned my back on the messenger, and opening the letter I read the following lines,

"Before I can write all I have to say, I must be sure of my messenger. I am boarding in a convent, and am very well treated, and I enjoy excellent health in spite of the anxiety of my mind. The superior has been instructed to forbid me all visitors and correspondence. I am, however, already certain of being able to write to you, notwithstanding these very strict orders. I entertain no doubt of your good faith, my beloved husband, and I feel sure that you will never doubt a heart which is wholly yours. Trust to me for the execution of whatever you may wish me to do, for I am yours and only yours. Answer only a few words until we are quite certain of our messenger.

"Muran, June 12th."

In less than three weeks my young friend had become a clever moralist; it is true that Love had been her teacher, and Love alone can work miracles. As I concluded the reading of her letter, I was in the state of a criminal pardoned at the foot of the scaffold. I required several minutes before I recovered the exercise of my will and my presence of mind.

I turned towards the messenger, and asked her if she could read.

"Ah, sir! if I could not read, it would be a great misfortune for me. There are seven women appointed for the service of the nuns of Muran. One of us comes in turn to Venice once a week; I come every Wednesday, and this day week I shall be able to bring you an answer to the letter which, if you like, you can write now."

"Then you can take charge of the letters entrusted to you by the nuns?"

"That is not supposed to be one of our duties but the faithful delivery of letters being the most important of the commissions committed to our care, we should not be trusted if we could not read the address of the letters placed in our hands. The nuns wanted to be sure that we shall not give to Peter the letter addressed to Paul. The good mothers are always afraid of our being guilty of such blunders. Therefore I shall be here again, without fail, this day week at the same hour, but please to order your servant to wake you in case you should be asleep, for our time is measured as if it were gold. Above all, rely entirely upon my discretion as long as you employ me; for if I did not know how to keep a silent tongue in my head I should lose my bread, and then what would become of me—a widow with four children, a boy eight years old, and three pretty girls, the eldest of whom is only sixteen? You can see them when you come to Muran. I live near the church, on the garden side, and I am always at home when I am not engaged in the service of the nuns, who are always sending me on one commission or another. The young lady—I do not know her name yet, for she has only been one week with us—gave me this letter, but so cleverly! Oh! she must be as witty as she is pretty, for three nuns who were there were completely bamboozled. She gave it to me with this other letter for myself, which I likewise leave in your hands. Poor child! she tells me to be discreet! She need not be afraid. Write to her, I entreat you, sir, that she can trust me, and answer boldly. I would not tell you to act in the same manner with all the other messengers of the convent, although I believe them to be honest—and God forbid I should speak ill of my fellow-creature—but they are all ignorant, you see; and it is certain that they babble, at least, with their confessors, if with nobody else. As for me, thank God! I know very well that I need not confess anything but my sins, and surely to carry a letter from a Christian woman to her brother in Christ is not a sin. Besides, my confessor is a good old monk, quite deaf, I believe, for the worthy man never answers me; but that is his business, not mine!"

I had not intended to ask her any questions, but if such had been my intention she would not have given me time to carry it into execution; and without my asking her anything, she was telling me everything I cared to know, and she did so in her anxiety for me to avail myself of her services exclusively.

I immediately sat down to write to my dear recluse, intending at first to write only a few lines, as she had requested me; but my time was too short to write so little. My letter was a screed of four pages, and very likely it said less than her note of one short page. I told her her letter had saved my life, and asked her whether I could hope to see her. I informed her that I had given a sequin to the messenger, that she would find another for herself under the seal of my letter, and that I would send her all the money she might want. I entreated her not to fail writing every Wednesday, to be certain that her letters would never be long enough to give me full particulars, not only of all she did, of all she was allowed to do, but also of all her thoughts respecting her release from imprisonment, and the overcoming of all the obstacles which were in the way of our mutual happiness; for I was as much hers as she was mine. I hinted to her the necessity of gaining the love of all the nuns and boarders, but without taking them into her confidence, and of shewing no dislike of her convent life. After praising her for the clever manner in which she had contrived to write to me, in spite of superior orders, I made her understand how careful she was to be to avoid being surprised while she was writing, because in such a case her room would certainly be searched and all her papers seized.

"Burn all my letters, darling," I added, "and recollect that you must go to confession often, but without implicating our love. Share with me all your sorrows, which interest me even more than your joys."

I sealed my letter in such a manner that no one could possibly guess that there was a sequin hidden under the sealing wax, and I rewarded the woman, promising her that I would give her the same reward every time that she brought me a letter from my friend. When she saw the sequin which I had put in her hand the good woman cried for joy, and she told me that, as the gates of the convent were never closed for her, she would deliver my letter the moment she found the young lady alone.

Here is the note which C— C— had given to the woman, with the letter addressed to me:

"God Himself, my good woman, prompts me to have confidence in you rather than in anybody else. Take this letter to Venice, and should the person to whom it is addressed not be in the city, bring it back to me. You must deliver it to that person himself, and if you find him you will most likely have an answer, which you must give me, but only when you are certain that nobody can see you."

If Love is imprudent, it is only in the hope of enjoyment; but when it is necessary to bring back happiness destroyed by some untoward accident, Love foresees all that the keenest perspicacity could possibly find out. The letter of my charming wife overwhelmed me with joy, and in one moment I passed from a state of despair to that of extreme felicity. I felt certain that I should succeed in carrying her off even if the walls of the convent could boast of artillery, and after the departure of the messenger my first thought was to endeavour to spend the seven days, before I could receive the second letter, pleasantly. Gambling alone could do it, but everybody had gone to Padua. I got my trunk ready, and immediately sent it to the burchiello then ready to start, and I left for Frusina. From that place I posted, and in less than three hours I arrived at the door of the Bragadin Palace, where I found my dear protector on the point of sitting down to dinner. He embraced me affectionately, and seeing me covered with perspiration he said to me,

"I am certain that you are in no hurry."

"No," I answered, "but I am starving."

I brought joy to the brotherly trio, and I enhanced their happiness when I told my friends that I would remain six days with them. De la Haye dined with us on that day; as soon as dinner was over he closeted himself with M. Dandoio, and for two hours they remained together. I had gone to bed during that time, but M. Dandolo came up to me and told me that I had arrived just in time to consult the oracle respecting an important affair entirely private to himself. He gave me the questions, and requested me to find the answers. He wanted to know whether he would act rightly if he accepted a project proposed to him by De la Haye.

The oracle answered negatively.

M. Dandolo, rather surprised, asked a second question: he wished Paralis to give his reasons for the denial.

I formed the cabalistic pile, and brought out this answer:

"I asked Casanova's opinion, and as I find it opposed to the proposal made by De la Haye, I do not wish to hear any more about it."

Oh! wonderful power of self-delusion! This worthy man, pleased at being able to throw the odium of a refusal on me, left me perfectly satisfied. I had no idea of the nature of the affair to which he had been alluding, and I felt no curiosity about it; but it annoyed me that a Jesuit should interfere and try to make my friends do anything otherwise than through my instrumentality, and I wanted that intriguer to know that my influence was greater than his own.

After that, I dressed, masked myself, and went to the opera, where I sat down to a faro-table and lost all my money. Fortune was determined to shew me that it does not always agree with love. My heart was heavy, I felt miserable; I went to bed. When I woke in the morning, I saw De la Haye come into my room with a beaming countenance, and, assuming an air of devoted friendship, he made a great show of his feelings towards me. I knew what to think of it all, and I waited for the 'denouement'.

"My dear friend," he said to me at last, "why did you dissuade M. Dandolo from doing what I had insinuated to him?"

"What had you insinuated to him?"

"You know well enough."

"If I knew it, I would not ask you!"

"M. Dandolo himself told me that you had advised him against it."

"Advised against, that may be, but certainly not dissuaded, for if he had been persuaded in his own mind he would not have asked my advice."

"As you please; but may I enquire your reasons?"

"Tell me first what your proposal was."

"Has he not told you?"

"Perhaps he has; but if you wish to know my reasons, I must hear the whole affair from your own lips, because M. Dandolo spoke to me under a promise of secrecy."

"Of what good is all this reserve?"

"Everyone has his own principles and his own way of thinking: I have a sufficiently good opinion of you to believe that you would act exactly as I do, for I have heard you say that in all secret matters one ought to guard against surprise."

"I am incapable of taking such an advantage of a friend; but as a general rule your maxim is a right one; I like prudence. I will tell you the whole affair. You are aware that Madame Tripolo has been left a widow, and that M. Dandolo is courting her assiduously, after having done the same for fourteen years during the life of the husband. The lady, who is still young, beautiful and lovely, and also is very respectable, wishes to become his wife. It is to me that she has confided her wishes, and as I saw nothing that was not praiseworthy, either in a temporal or in a spiritual point of view, in that union, for after all we are all men, I took the affair in hand with real pleasure. I fancied even that M. Dandolo felt some inclination for that marriage when he told me that he would give me his decision this morning. I am not astonished at his having asked your advice in such an important affair, for a prudent man is right in asking the opinion of a wise friend before taking a decisive step; but I must tell you candidly that I am astonished at your disapproval of such a marriage. Pray excuse me if, in order to improve by the information, I ask why your opinion is exactly the reverse of mine."

Delighted at having discovered the whole affair, at having arrived in time to prevent my friend who was goodness itself contracting an absurd marriage, I answered the hypocrite that I loved M. Dandolo, that I knew his temperament, and that I was certain that a marriage with a woman like Madame Tripolo would shorten his life.

"That being my opinion," I added, "you must admit that as a true friend I was right in advising him against your proposal. Do you recollect having told me that you never married for the very same reason? Do you recollect your strong arguments in favour of celibacy while we were at Parma? Consider also, I beg, that every man has a certain small stock of selfishness, and that I may be allowed to have mine when I think that if M. Dandolo took a wife the influence of that wife would of course have some weight, and that the more she gained in influence over him the more I should lose. So you see it would not be natural for me to advise him to take a step which would ultimately prove very detrimental to my interests. If you can prove that my reasons are either trifling or sophistical, speak openly: I will tell M. Dandolo that my mind has changed; Madame Tripolo will become his wife when we return to Venice. But let me warn you that thorough conviction can alone move me."

"I do not believe myself clever enough to convince you. I shall write to Madame Tripolo that she must apply to you."

"Do not write anything of the sort to that lady, or she will think that you are laughing at her. Do you suppose her foolish enough to expect that I will give way to her wishes? She knows that I do not like her."

"How can she possibly know that?"

"She must have remarked that I have never cared to accompany M. Dandolo to her house. Learn from me once for all, that as long as I live with my three friends they shall have no wife but me. You may get married as soon as you please; I promise not to throw any obstacle in your way; but if you wish to remain on friendly terms with me give up all idea of leading my three friends astray."

"You are very caustic this morning."

"I lost all my money last night.

"Then I have chosen a bad time. Farewell."

From that day, De la Haye became my secret enemy, and to him I was in a great measure indebted, two years later, for my imprisonment under The Leads of Venice; not owing to his slanders, for I do not believe he was capable of that, Jesuit though he was—and even amongst such people there is sometimes some honourable feeling—but through the mystical insinuations which he made in the presence of bigoted persons. I must give fair notice to my readers that, if they are fond of such people, they must not read these Memoirs, for they belong to a tribe which I have good reason to attack unmercifully.

The fine marriage was never again alluded to. M. Dandolo continued to visit his beautiful widow every day, and I took care to elicit from Paralis a strong interdiction ever to put my foot in her house.

Don Antonio Croce, a young Milanese whom I had known in Reggio, a confirmed gambler, and a downright clever hand in securing the favours of Dame Fortune, called on me a few minutes after De la Haye had retired. He told me that, having seen me lose all my money the night before, he had come to offer me the means of retrieving my losses, if I would take an equal interest with him in a faro bank that he meant to hold at his house, and in which he would have as punters seven or eight rich foreigners who were courting his wife.

"If you will put three hundred sequins in my bank," he added, "you shall be my partner. I have three hundred sequins myself, but that is not enough because the punters play high. Come and dine at my house, and you will make their acquaintance. We can play next Friday as there will be no opera, and you may rely upon our winning plenty of gold, for a certain Gilenspetz, a Swede, may lose twenty thousand sequins."

I was without any resources, or at all events I could expect no assistance except from M. de Bragadin upon whom I felt ashamed of encroaching. I was well aware that the proposal made by Croce was not strictly moral, and that I might have chosen a more honourable society; but if I had refused, the purse of Madame Croce's admirers would not have been more mercifully treated; another would have profited by that stroke of good fortune. I was therefore not rigid enough to refuse my assistance as adjutant and my share of the pie; I accepted Croce's invitation.

V

I Get Rich Again—My Adventure At Dolo—Analysis of a
Long Letter From C. C.—Mischievous Trick Played Upon Me
By P. C.—At Vincenza—A Tragi-comedy At the Inn

Necessity, that imperious law and my only excuse, having made
me almost the partner of a cheat, there was still the difficulty of
finding the three hundred sequins required; but I postponed the task
of finding them until after I should have made the acquaintance of the
dupes of the goddess to whom they addressed their worship. Croce took
me to the Prato delta Valle, where we found madame surrounded with
foreigners. She was pretty; and as a secretary of the imperial ambassador,
Count Rosemberg, had attached himself to her, not one of the Venetian
nobles dared court her. Those who interested me among the satellites
gravitating around that star were the Swede Gilenspetz, a Hamburger,
the Englishman Mendez, who has already been mentioned, and three
or four others to whore Croce called my attention.

We dined all together, and after dinner there was a general call for a
faro bank; but Croce did not accept. His refusal surprised me, because
with three hundred sequins, being a very skilful player, he had enough
to try his fortune. He did not, however, allow my suspicions to last
long, for he took me to his own room and shewed me fifty pieces of
eight, which were equal to three hundred sequins. When I saw that
the professional gambler had not chosen me as his partner with the
intention of making a dupe of me, I told him that I would certainly
procure the amount, and upon that promise he invited everybody to
supper for the following day. We agreed that we would divide the spoils
before parting in the evening, and that no one should be allowed to
play on trust.

I had to procure the amount, but to whom could I apply? I could
ask no one but M. de Bragadin. The excellent man had not that sum
in his possession, for his purse was generally empty; but he found a
usurer—a species of animal too numerous unfortunately for young
men—who, upon a note of hand endorsed by him, gave me a thousand
ducats, at five per cent. for one month, the said interest being deducted
by anticipation from the capital. It was exactly the amount I required.
I went to the supper; Croce held the bank until daylight, and we

divided sixteen hundred sequins between us. The game continued the next evening, and Gilenspetz alone lost two thousand sequins; the Jew Mendez lost about one thousand. Sunday was sanctified by rest, but on Monday the bank won four thousand sequins. On the Tuesday we all dined together, and the play was resumed; but we had scarcely begun when an officer of the podesta made his appearance and informed Croce that he wanted a little private conversation with him. They left the room together, and after a short absence Croce came back rather crestfallen; he announced that by superior orders he was forbidden to hold a bank at his house. Madame fainted away, the punters hurried out, and I followed their example, as soon as I had secured one-half of the gold which was on the table. I was glad enough it was not worse. As I left, Croce told me that we would meet again in Venice, for he had been ordered to quit Padua within twenty-four hours. I expected it would be so, because he was to well known; but his greatest crime, in the opinion of the podesta, was that he attracted the players to his own house, whilst the authorities wanted all the lovers of play to lose their money at the opera, where the bankers were mostly noblemen from Venice.

I left the city on horseback in the evening and in very bad weather, but nothing could have kept me back, because early the next morning I expected a letter from my dear prisoner. I had only travelled six miles from Padua when my horse fell, and I found my left leg caught under it. My boots were soft ones, and I feared I had hurt myself. The postillion was ahead of me, but hearing the noise made by the fall he came up and disengaged me; I was not hurt, but my horse was lame. I immediately took the horse of the postillion, to which I was entitled, but the insolent fellow getting hold of the bit refused to let me proceed. I tried to make him understand that he was wrong; but, far from giving way to my arguments, he persisted in stopping me, and being in a great hurry to continue my journey I fired one of my pistols in his face, but without touching him. Frightened out of his wits, the man let go, and I galloped off. When I reached the Dolo, I went straight to the stables, and I myself saddled a horse which a postillion, to whom I gave a crown, pointed out to me as being excellent. No one thought of being astonished at my other postillion having remained behind, and we started at full speed. It was then one o'clock in the morning; the storm had broken up the road, and the night was so dark that I could not see anything within a yard ahead of me; the day was breaking when we arrived in Fusina.

GIACOMO CASANOVA

The boatmen threatened me with a fresh storm; but setting everything at defiance I took a four-oared boat, and reached my dwelling quite safe but shivering with cold and wet to the skin. I had scarcely been in my room for a quarter of an hour when the messenger from Muran presented herself and gave me a letter, telling me that she would call for the answer in two hours. That letter was a journal of seven pages, the faithful translation of which might weary my readers, but here is the substance of it:

After the interview with M. de Bragadin, the father of C— C— had gone home, had his wife and daughter to his room, and enquired kindly from the last where she had made my acquaintance. She answered that she had seen me five or six times in her brother's room, that I had asked her whether she would consent to be my wife, and that she had told me that she was dependent upon her father and mother. The father had then said that she was too young to think of marriage, and besides, I had not yet conquered a position in society. After that decision he repaired to his son's room, and locked the small door inside as well as the one communicating with the apartment of the mother, who was instructed by him to let me believe that she had gone to the country, in case I should call on her.

Two days afterwards he came to C— C—, who was beside her sick mother, and told her that her aunt would take her to a convent, where she was to remain until a husband had been provided for her by her parents. She answered that, being perfectly disposed to submit to his will, she would gladly obey him. Pleased with her ready obedience he promised to go and see her, and to let his mother visit her likewise, as soon as her health was better. Immediately after that conversation the aunt had called for her, and a gondola had taken them to the convent, where she had been ever since. Her bed and her clothes had been brought to her; she was well pleased with her room and with the nun to whom she had been entrusted, and under whose supervision she was. It was by her that she had been forbidden to receive either letters or visits, or to write to anybody, under penalty of excommunication from the Holy Father, of everlasting damnation, and of other similar trifles; yet the same nun had supplied her with paper, ink and books, and it was at night that my young friend transgressed the laws of the convent in order to write all these particulars to me. She expressed her conviction respecting the discretion and the faithfulness of the messenger, and she thought that she would remain devoted, because, being poor, our sequins were a little fortune for her.

She related to me in the most assuring manner that the handsomest of all the nuns in the convent loved her to distraction, gave her a French lesson twice a-day, and had amicably forbidden her to become acquainted with the other boarders. That nun was only twenty-two years of age; she was beautiful, rich and generous; all the other nuns shewed her great respect. "When we are alone," wrote my friend, "she kisses me so tenderly that you would be jealous if she were not a woman." As to our project of running away, she did not think it would be very difficult to carry it into execution, but that it would be better to wait until she knew the locality better. She told me to remain faithful and constant, and asked me to send her my portrait hidden in a ring by a secret spring known only to us. She added that I might send it to her by her mother, who had recovered her usual health, and was in the habit of attending early mass at her parish church every day by herself. She assured me that the excellent woman would be delighted to see me, and to do anything I might ask her. "At all events," she concluded, "I hope to find myself in a few months in a position which will scandalize the convent if they are obstinately bent upon keeping me here."

I was just finishing my answer when Laura, the messenger, returned for it. After I had paid the sequin I had promised her, I gave her a parcel containing sealing-wax, paper, pens, and a tinder-box, which she promised to deliver to C— C—. My darling had told her that I was her cousin, and Laura feigned to believe it.

Not knowing what to do in Venice, and believing that I ought for the sake of my honour to shew myself in Padua, or else people might suppose that I had received the same order as Croce, I hurried my breakfast, and procured a 'bolletta' from the booking-office for Rome; because I foresaw that the firing of my pistol and the lame horse might not have improved the temper of the post-masters; but by shewing them what is called in Italy a 'bolletta', I knew that they could not refuse to supply me with horses whenever they had any in their stables. As far as the pistol-shot was concerned I had no fear, for I had purposely missed the insolent postillion; and even if I had killed him on the spot it would not have been of much importance.

In Fusina I took a two-wheeled chaise, for I was so tired that I could not have performed the journey on horseback, and I reached the Dolo, where I was recognized and horses were refused me.

I made a good deal of noise, and the post-master, coming out, threatened to have me arrested if I did not pay him for his dead horse.

I answered that if the horse were dead I would account for it to the postmaster in Padua, but what I wanted was fresh horses without delay.

And I shewed him the dread 'bolletta', the sight of which made him lower his tone; but he told me that, even if he supplied me with horses, I had treated the postillion so badly that not one of his men would drive me. "If that is the case," I answered, "you shall accompany me yourself." The fellow laughed in my face, turned his back upon me, and went away. I took two witnesses, and I called with them at the office of a public notary, who drew up a properly-worded document, by which I gave notice to the post-master that I should expect an indemnity of ten sequins for each hour of delay until I had horses supplied to me.

As soon as he had been made acquainted with the contents of this, he gave orders to bring out two restive horses. I saw at once that his intention was to have me upset along the road, and perhaps thrown into the river; but I calmly told the postillion that at the very moment my chaise was upset I would blow his brains out with a pistol-shot; this threat frightened the man; he took his horses back to the stables, and declared to his master that he would not drive me. At that very moment a courier arrived, who called for six carriage horses and two saddle ones. I warned the post-master that no one should leave the place before me, and that if he opposed my will there would be a sanguinary contest; in order to prove that I was in earnest I took out my pistols. The fellow began to swear, but, everyone saying that he was in the wrong, he disappeared.

Five minutes afterwards whom should I see, arriving in a beautiful berlin drawn by six horses, but Croce with his wife, a lady's maid, and two lackeys in grand livery. He alighted, we embraced one another, and I told him, assuming an air of sadness, that he could not leave before me. I explained how the case stood; he said I was right, scolded loudly, as if he had been a great lord, and made everybody tremble. The postmaster had disappeared; his wife came and ordered the postillions to attend to my wants. During that time Croce said to me that I was quite right in going back to Padua, where the public rumour had spread the report of my having left the city in consequence of an order from the police. He informed me that the podesta had likewise expelled M. de Gondoin, a colonel in the service of the Duke of Modena, because he held a faro bank at his house. I promised him to pay him a visit in Venice in the ensuing week. Croce, who had dropped from the sky to assist me in a moment of great distress, had won ten thousand sequins in four evenings: I had received five thousand for my share; and lost no time in paying my debts and in redeeming all the articles which I had been compelled to pledge. That scamp brought me back the smiles of Fortune, and from that moment I got rid of the ill luck which had seemed to fasten on me.

I reached Padua in safety, and the postillion, who very likely out of fear had driven me in good style, was well pleased with my liberality; it was the best way of making peace with the tribe. My arrival caused great joy to my three friends, whom my sudden departure had alarmed, with the exception of M. de Bragadin, in whose hands I had placed my cash-box the day before. His two friends had given credence to the general report, stating that the podesta had ordered me to leave Padua. They forgot that I was a citizen of Venice, and that the podesta could not pass such a sentence upon me without exposing himself to legal proceedings. I was tired, but instead of going to bed I dressed myself in my best attire in order to go to the opera without a mask. I told my friends that it was necessary for me to shew myself, so as to give the lie to all that had been reported about me by slandering tongues. De la Haye said to me,

"I shall be delighted if all those reports are false; but you have no one to blame but yourself, for your hurried departure gave sufficient cause for all sorts of surmises."

"And for slander."

"That may be; but people want to know everything, and they invent when they cannot guess the truth."

"And evil-minded fools lose no time in repeating those inventions everywhere."

"But there can be no doubt that you wanted to kill the postillion. Is that a calumny likewise?"

"The greatest of all. Do you think that a good shot can miss a man when he is firing in his very face, unless he does it purposely?"

"It seems difficult; but at all events it is certain that the horse is dead, and you must pay for it."

"No, sir, not even if the horse belonged to you, for the postillion preceded me. You know a great many things; do you happen to know the posting regulations? Besides, I was in a great hurry because I had promised a pretty woman to breakfast with her, and such engagements, as you are well aware, cannot be broken."

Master de la Haye looked angry at the rather caustic irony with which I had sprinkled the dialogue; but he was still more vexed when, taking some gold out of my pocket, I returned to him the sum he had lent me in Vienna. A man never argues well except when his purse is well filled; then his spirits are pitched in a high key, unless he should happen to be stupefied by some passion raging in his soul.

M. de Bragadin thought I was quite right to shew myself at the opera without a mask.

The moment I made my appearance in the pit everybody seemed quite astonished, and I was overwhelmed with compliments, sincere or not. After the first ballet I went to the card-room, and in four deals I won five hundred sequins. Starving, and almost dead for want of sleep, I returned to my friends to boast of my victory. My friend Bavois was there, and he seized the opportunity to borrow from me fifty sequins, which he never returned; true, I never asked him for them.

My thoughts being constantly absorbed in my dear C— C—, I spent the whole of the next day in having my likeness painted in miniature by a skilful Piedmontese, who had come for the Fair of Padua, and who in after times made a great deal of money in Venice. When he had completed my portrait he painted for me a beautiful St. Catherine of the same size, and a clever Venetian jeweller made the ring, the bezel of which shewed only the sainted virgin; but a blue spot, hardly visible on the white enamel which surrounded it, corresponded with the secret spring which brought out my portrait, and the change was obtained by pressing on the blue spot with the point of a pin.

On the following Friday, as we were rising from the dinner-table, a letter was handed to me. It was with great surprise that I recognized the writing of P— C—. He asked me to pay him a visit at the "Star Hotel," where he would give me some interesting information. Thinking that he might have something to say concerning his sister, I went to him at once.

I found him with Madame C—, and after congratulating him upon his release from prison I asked him for the news he had to communicate.

"I am certain," he said, "that my sister is in a convent, and I shall be able to tell you the name of it when I return to Venice."

"You will oblige me," I answered, pretending not to know anything.

But his news had only been a pretext to make me come to him, and his eagerness to communicate it had a very different object in view than the gratification of my curiosity.

"I have sold," he said to me, "my privileged contract for three years for a sum of fifteen thousand florins, and the man with whom I have made the bargain took me out of prison by giving security for me, and advanced me six thousand florins in four letters of exchange."

He shewed me the letters of exchange, endorsed by a name which I did not know, but which he said was a very good one, and he continued,

"I intend to buy six thousand florins worth of silk goods from the looms of Vicenza, and to give in payment to the merchants these letters of exchange. I am certain of selling those goods rapidly with a profit of ten per cent. Come with us to Vicenza; I will give you some of my goods to the amount of two hundred sequins, and thus you will find yourself covered for the guarantee which you have been kind enough to give to the jeweller for the ring. We shall complete the transaction within twenty-four hours."

I did not feel much inclination for the trip, but I allowed myself to be blinded by the wish to cover the amount which I had guaranteed, and which I had no doubt I would be called upon to pay some day or other.

"If I do not go with him," I said to myself "he will sell the goods at a loss of twenty-five per cent. and I shall get nothing."

I promised to accompany him. He shewed me several letters of recommendation for the best houses in Vicenza, and our departure was fixed for early the next morning. I was at the "Star Hotel" by daybreak. A carriage and four was ready; the hotel-keeper came up with his bill, and P— C— begged me to pay it. The bill amounted to five sequins; four of which had been advanced in cash by the landlord to pay the driver who had brought them from Fusina. I saw that it was a put-up thing, yet I paid with pretty good grace, for I guessed that the scoundrel had left Venice without a penny. We reached Vicenza in three hours, and we put up at the "Cappello," where P— C— ordered a good dinner before leaving me with the lady to call upon the manufacturers.

When the beauty found herself alone with me, she began by addressing friendly reproaches to me.

"I have loved you," she said, "for eighteen years; the first time that I saw you we were in Padua, and we were then only nine years old."

I certainly had no recollection of it. She was the daughter of the antiquarian friend of M. Grimani, who had placed me as a boarder with the accursed Sclavonian woman. I could not help smiling, for I recollected that her mother had loved me.

Shop-boys soon began to make their appearance, bringing pieces of goods, and the face of Madame C— brightened up. In less than two hours the room was filled with them, and P— C— came back with two merchants, whom he had invited to dinner. Madame allured them by her pretty manners; we dined, and exquisite wines were drunk in profusion. In the afternoon fresh goods were brought in; P— C— made a list of them with the prices; but he wanted more, and the merchants promised to send them the next day, although it was Sunday. Towards the evening several counts arrived, for in Vicenza every nobleman is a count. P— C— had left his letters of recommendation at their houses. We had a Count Velo, a Count Sesso, a Count Trento—all very amiable companions. They invited us to accompany them to the casino, where Madame C— shone by her charms and her coquettish manners. After we had spent two hours in that place, P— C— invited all his new friends to supper, and it was a scene of gaiety and profusion. The whole affair annoyed me greatly, and therefore I was not amiable; the consequence was that no one spoke to me. I rose from my seat and went to bed, leaving the joyous company still round the festive board. In the morning I came downstairs, had my breakfast, and looked about me. The room was so full of goods that I did not see how P— C— could possibly pay for all with his six thousand florins. He told me, however, that his business would be completed on the morrow, and that we were invited to a ball where all the nobility would be present. The merchants with whom he had dealt came to dine with us, and the dinner was remarkable for its extreme profusion.

We went to the ball; but I soon got very weary of it, for every body was speaking to Madame C— and to P— C—, who never uttered a word with any meaning, but whenever I opened my lips people would pretend not to hear me. I invited a lady to dance a minuet; she accepted, but she looked constantly to the right or to the left, and seemed to consider me as a mere dancing machine. A quadrille was formed, but the thing was contrived in such a manner as to leave me out of it, and the very lady who had refused me as a partner danced with another gentleman. Had I been in good spirits I should certainly have resented such conduct, but I preferred to leave the ball-room. I went to bed, unable to understand why the nobility of Vicenza treated me in such a way. Perhaps they neglected me because I was not named in the letters of introduction given to P— C—, but I thought that they might have known the laws of common politeness. I bore the evil patiently, however, as we were to leave the city the next day.

On Monday, the worthy pair being tired, they slept until noon, and after dinner P— C— went out to pay for the goods.

We were to go away early on the Tuesday, and I instinctively longed for that moment. The counts whom P— C— had invited were delighted with his mistress, and they came to supper; but I avoided meeting them.

On the Tuesday morning I was duly informed that breakfast was ready, but as I did not answer the summons quickly enough the servant came up again, and told me that my wife requested me to make haste. Scarcely had the word "wife" escaped his lips than I visited the cheek of the poor fellow with a tremendous smack, and in my rage kicked him downstairs, the bottom of which he reached in four springs, to the imminent risk of his neck. Maddened with rage I entered the breakfast-room, and addressing myself to P— C—, I asked him who was the scoundrel who had announced me in the hotel as the husband of Madame C—. He answered that he did not know; but at the same moment the landlord came into the room with a big knife in his hand, and asked me why I had kicked his servant down the stairs. I quickly drew a pistol, and threatening him with it I demanded imperatively from him the name of the person who had represented me as the husband of that woman.

"Captain P— C—," answered the landlord, "gave the names, profession, etc., of your party."

At this I seized the impudent villain by the throat, and pinning him against the wall with a strong hand I would have broken his head with the butt of my pistol, if the landlord had not prevented me. Madame had pretended to swoon, for those women can always command tears or fainting fits, and the cowardly P— C— kept on saying,

"It is not true, it is not true!"

The landlord ran out to get the hotel register, and he angrily thrust it under the nose of the coward, daring him to deny his having dictated: Captain P— C—, with M. and Madame Casanova. The scoundrel answered that his words had certainly not been heard rightly, and the incensed landlord slapped the book in his face with such force that he sent him rolling, almost stunned, against the wall.

When I saw that the wretched poltroon was receiving such degrading treatment without remembering that he had a sword hanging by his side, I left the room, and asked the landlord to order me a carriage to take me to Padua.

Beside myself with rage, blushing for very shame, seeing but too late the fault I had committed by accepting the society of a scoundrel, I went up to my room, and hurriedly packed up my carpet-bag. I was just going out when Madame C— presented herself before me.

"Begone, madam," I said to her, "or, in my rage, I might forget the respect due to your sex."

She threw herself, crying bitterly, on a chair, entreated me to forgive her, assuring me that she was innocent, and that she was not present when the knave had given the names. The landlady, coming in at that moment, vouched for the truth of her assertion. My anger began to abate, and as I passed near the window I saw the carriage I had ordered waiting for me with a pair of good horses. I called for the landlord in order to pay whatever my share of the expense might come to, but he told me that as I had ordered nothing myself I had nothing to pay. Just at that juncture Count Velo came in.

"I daresay, count," I said, "that you believe this woman to be my wife."

"That is a fact known to everybody in the city."

"Damnation! And you have believed such a thing, knowing that I occupy this room alone, and seeing me leave the ball-room and the supper-table yesterday alone, leaving her with you all!"

"Some husbands are blessed with such easy dispositions!"

"I do not think I look like one of that species, and you are not a judge of men of honour, let us go out, and I undertake to prove it to you."

The count rushed down the stairs and out of the hotel. The miserable C— was choking, and I could not help pitying her; for a woman has in her tears a weapon which through my life I have never known to resist. I considered that if I left the hotel without paying anything, people might laugh at my anger and suppose that I had a share in the swindle; I requested the landlord to bring me the account, intending to pay half of it. He went for it, but another scene awaited me. Madame C—, bathed in tears, fell on her knees, and told me that if I abandoned her she was lost, for she had no money and nothing to leave as security for her hotel bill.

"What, madam! Have you not letters of exchange to the amount of six thousand florins, or the goods bought with them?"

"The goods are no longer here; they have all been taken away, because the letters of exchange, which you saw, and which we considered as good as cash, only made the merchants laugh; they have sent for everything. Oh! who could have supposed it?"

"The scoundrel! He knew it well enough, and that is why he was so anxious to bring me here. Well, it is right that I should pay the penalty of my own folly."

The bill brought by the landlord amounted to forty sequins, a very high figure for three days; but a large portion of that sum was cash advanced by the landlord, I immediately felt that my honour demanded that I should pay the bill in full; and I paid without any hesitation, taking care to get a receipt given in the presence of two witnesses. I then made a present of two sequins to the nephew of the landlord to console him for the thrashing he had received, and I refused the same sum to the wretched C——, who had sent the landlady to beg it for her.

Thus ended that unpleasant adventure, which taught me a lesson, and a lesson which I ought not to have required. Two or three weeks later, I heard that Count Trento had given those two miserable beings some money to enable them to leave the city; as far as I was concerned, I would not have anything to do with them. A month afterwards P—— C—— was again arrested for debt, the man who had been security for him having become a bankrupt. He had the audacity to write a long letter to me, entreating me to go and see him, but I did not answer him. I was quite as inflexible towards Madame C——, whom I always refused to see. She was reduced to great poverty.

I returned to Padua, where I stopped only long enough to take my ring and to dine with M. de Bragadin, who went back to Venice a few days afterwards.

The messenger from the convent brought me a letter very early in the morning; I devoured its contents; it was very loving, but gave no news. In my answer I gave my dear C—— C—— the particulars of the infamous trick played upon me by her villainous brother, and mentioned the ring, with the secret of which I acquainted her.

According to the information I had received from C—— C——, I placed myself, one morning, so as to see her mother enter the church, into which I followed her. Kneeling close to her, I told her that I wished to speak with her, and she followed me to the cloister. I began by speaking a few consoling words; then I told her that I would remain faithful to her daughter, and I asked her whether she visited her.

"I intend," she said, "to go and kiss my dear child next Sunday, and I shall of course speak of you with her, for I know well enough that she will be delighted to have news of you; but to my great regret I am not at liberty to tell you where she is."

"I do not wish you to tell me, my good mother, but allow me to send her this ring by you. It is the picture of her patroness, and I wish you to entreat her to wear it always on her finger; tell her to look at the image during her daily prayers, for without that protection she can never become my wife. Tell her that, on my side, I address every day a credo to St. James."

Delighted with the piety of my feelings and with the prospect of recommending this new devotion to her daughter, the good woman promised to fulfil my commission. I left her, but not before I had placed in her hand ten sequins which I begged her to force upon her daughter's acceptance to supply herself with the trifles she might require. She accepted, but at the same time she assured me that her father had taken care to provide her with all necessaries. The letter which I received from C— C—, on the following Wednesday, was the expression of the most tender affection and the most lively gratitude. She said that the moment she was alone nothing could be more rapid than the point of the pin which made St. Catherine cut a somersault, and presented to her eager eyes the beloved features of the being who was the whole world to her. "I am constantly kissing you," she added, "even when some of the nuns are looking at me, for whenever they come near me I have only to let the top part of the ring fall back and my dear patroness takes care to conceal everything. All the nuns are highly pleased with my devotion and with the confidence I have in the protection of my blessed patroness, whom they think very much like me in the face." It was nothing but a beautiful face created by the fancy of the painter, but my dear little wife was so lovely that beauty was sure to be like her.

She said, likewise, that the nun who taught her French had offered her fifty sequins for the ring on account of the likeness between her and the portrait of the saint, but not out of veneration for her patroness, whom she turned into ridicule as she read her life. She thanked me for the ten sequins I had sent her, because, her mother having given them to her in the presence of several of the sisters, she was thus enabled to spend a little money without raising the suspicions of those curious and inquisitive nuns. She liked to offer trifling presents to the other boarders, and the money allowed her to gratify that innocent taste.

"My mother," added she, "praised your piety very highly; she is delighted with your feelings of devotion. Never mention again, I beg, the name of my unworthy brother."

For five or six weeks her letters were full of the blessed St. Catherine, who caused her to tremble with fear every time she found herself compelled to trust the ring to the mystic curiosity of the elderly nuns, who, in order to see the likeness better through their spectacles, brought it close to their eyes, and rubbed the enamel. "I am in constant fear," C— C— wrote, "of their pressing the invisible blue spot by chance. What would become of me, if my patroness, jumping up, discovered to their eyes a face—very divine, it is true, but which is not at all like that of a saint? Tell me, what could I do in such a case?"

One month after the second arrest of P— C—, the jeweller, who had taken my security for the ring, called on me for payment of the bill. I made an arrangement with him; and on condition of my giving him twenty sequins, and leaving him every right over the debtor, he exonerated me. From his prison the impudent P— C— harassed me with his cowardly entreaties for alms and assistance.

Croce was in Venice, and engrossed a great share of the general attention. He kept a fine house, an excellent table, and a faro bank with which he emptied the pockets of his dupes. Foreseeing what would happen sooner or later, I had abstained from visiting him at his house, but we were friendly whenever we met. His wife having been delivered of a boy, Croce asked me to stand as god-father, a favour which I thought I could grant; but after the ceremony and the supper which was the consequence of it, I never entered the house of my former partner, and I acted rightly. I wish I had always been as prudent in my conduct.

VI

CROCE IS EXPELLED FROM VENICE—SGOMBRO—HIS INFAMY
AND DEATH—MISFORTUNE WHICH BEFALLS MY DEAR
C. C.—I RECEIVE AN ANONYMOUS LETTER FROM A NUN,
AND ANSWER IT—AN AMOROUS INTRIGUE

My former partner was, as I have said before, a skilful and experienced hand at securing the favours of Fortune; he was driving a good trade in Venice, and as he was amiable, and what is called in society a gentleman, he might have held that excellent footing for a long time, if he had been satisfied with gambling; for the State Inquisitors would have too much to attend to if they wished to compel fools to spare their fortunes, dupes to be prudent, and cheats not to dupe the fools; but, whether through the folly of youth or through a vicious disposition, the cause of his exile was of an extraordinary and disgusting nature.

A Venetian nobleman, noble by birth, but very ignoble in his propensities, called Sgombro, and belonging to the Gritti family, fell deeply in love with him, and Croce, either for fun or from taste, shewed himself very compliant. Unfortunately the reserve commanded by common decency was not a guest at their amorous feats, and the scandal became so notorious that the Government was compelled to notify to Croce the order to quit the city, and to seek his fortune in some other place.

Some time afterwards the infamous Sgombro seduced his own two sons, who were both very young, and, unfortunately for him, he put the youngest in such a state as to render necessary an application to a surgeon. The infamous deed became publicly known, and the poor child confessed that he had not had the courage to refuse obedience to his father. Such obedience was, as a matter of course, not considered as forming a part of the duties which a son owes to his father, and the State Inquisitors sent the disgusting wretch to the citadel of Cataro, where he died after one year of confinement.

It is well known that the air of Cataro is deadly, and that the Tribunal sentences to inhale it only such criminals as are not judged publicly for fear of exciting too deeply the general horror by the publication of the trial.

It was to Cataro that the Council of Ten sent, fifteen years ago, the celebrated advocate Cantarini, a Venetian nobleman, who by his eloquence had made himself master of the great Council, and was on the point of changing the constitution of the State. He died there at the end of the year. As for his accomplices, the Tribunal thought that it was enough to punish the four or five leaders, and to pretend not to know the others, who through fear of punishment returned silently to their allegiance.

That Sgombro, of whom I spoke before, had a charming wife who is still alive, I believe. Her name was Cornelia Gitti; she was as celebrated by her wit as by her beauty, which she kept in spite of her years. Having recovered her liberty through the death of her husband, she knew better than to make herself a second time the prisoner of the Hymenean god; she loved her independence too much; but as she loved pleasure too, she accepted the homage of the lovers who pleased her taste.

One Monday, towards the end of July, my servant woke me at daybreak to tell me that Laura wished to speak to me. I foresaw some misfortune, and ordered the servant to shew her in immediately. These are the contents of the letter which she handed to me:

"My dearest, a misfortune has befallen me last evening, and it makes me very miserable because I must keep it a secret from everyone in the convent. I am suffering from a very severe loss of blood, and I do not know what to do, having but very little linen. Laura tells me I shall require a great deal of it if the flow of blood continues. I can take no one into my confidence but you, and I entreat you to send me as much linen as you can. You see that I have been compelled to make a confidante of Laura, who is the only person allowed to enter my room at all times. If I should die, my dear husband, everybody in the convent would, of course, know the cause of my death; but I think of you, and I shudder. What will you do in your grief? Ah, darling love! what a pity!"

I dressed myself hurriedly, plying Laura with questions all the time. She told me plainly that it was a miscarriage, and that it was necessary to act with great discretion in order to save the reputation of my young friend; that after all she required nothing but plenty of linen, and that it would be nothing. Commonplace words of consolation, which did not allay the fearful anxiety under which I was labouring. I went out with Laura, called on a Jew from whom I bought a quantity of sheets and two hundred napkins and, putting it all in a large bag, I repaired with her to Muran. On our way there I wrote in pencil to my sweetheart, telling her to have entire confidence in Laura, and assuring her that I would not leave Muran until all danger had passed. Before we landed, Laura told me that, in order not to be remarked, I had better conceal myself in her house. At any other time it would have been shutting up the wolf in the sheep-fold. She left me in a miserable-looking small room on the ground floor, and concealing about herself as much linen as she could she hurried to her patient, whom she had not seen since the previous evening. I was in hopes that she would find her out of danger, and I longed to see her come back with that good news.

She was absent about one hour, and when she returned her looks were sad. She told me that my poor friend, having lost a great deal of blood during the night, was in bed in a very weak state, and that all we could do was to pray to God for her, because, if the flooding of the blood did not stop soon, she could not possibly live twenty-four hours.

When I saw the linen which she had concealed under her clothes to bring it out, I could not disguise my horror, and I thought the sight would kill me. I fancied myself in a slaughter-house! Laura, thinking of consoling me, told me that I could rely upon the secret being well kept.

"Ah! what do I care!" I exclaimed. "Provided she lives, let the whole world know that she is my wife!"

At any other time, the foolishness of poor Laura would have made me laugh; but in such a sad moment I had neither the inclination nor the courage to be merry.

"Our dear patient," added Laura, "smiled as she was reading your letter, and she said that, with you so near her, she was certain not to die."

Those words did me good, but a man needs so little to console him or to soothe his grief.

"When the nuns are at their dinner," said Laura, "I will go back to the convent with as much linen as I can conceal about me, and in the mean time I am going to wash all this."

"Has she had any visitors?"

"Oh, yes! all the convent; but no one has any suspicion of the truth."

"But in such hot weather as this she can have only a very light blanket over her, and her visitors must remark the great bulk of the napkins."

"There is no fear of that, because she is sitting up in her bed."

"What does she eat?"

"Nothing, for she must not eat."

Soon afterwards Laura went out, and I followed her. I called upon a physician, where I wasted my time and my money, in order to get from him a long prescription which was useless, for it would have put all the convent in possession of the secret, or, to speak more truly, her secret would have been known to the whole world, for a secret known to a nun soon escapes out of the convent's walls. Besides, the physician of the convent himself would most likely have betrayed it through a spirit of revenge.

I returned sadly to my miserable hole in Laura's house. Half an hour afterwards she came to me, crying bitterly, and she placed in my hands this letter, which was scarcely legible:

"I have not strength enough to write to you, my darling; I am getting weaker and weaker; I am losing all my blood, and I am afraid there is no remedy. I abandon myself to the will of God, and I thank Him for having saved me from dishonour. Do not make yourself unhappy. My only consolation is to know that you are near me. Alas! if I could see you but for one moment I would die happy."

The sight of a dozen napkins brought by Laura made me shudder, and the good woman imagined that she afforded me some consolation by telling me that as much linen could be soaked with a bottle of blood. My mind was not disposed to taste such consolation; I was in despair, and I addressed to myself the fiercest reproaches, upbraiding myself as the cause of the death of that adorable creature. I threw myself on the bed, and remained there, almost stunned, for more than six hours, until Laura's return from the convent with twenty napkins entirely soaked. Night had come on, and she could not go back to her patient until morning. I passed a fearful night without food, without sleep, looking upon myself with horror, and refusing all the kind attentions that Laura's daughters tried to shew me.

It was barely daylight when Laura same to announce to me, in the saddest tone, that my poor friend did not bleed any more. I thought she was dead, and I screamed loudly,

"Oh! she is no more!"

"She is still breathing, sir; but I fear she will not outlive this day, for she is worn out. She can hardly open her eyes, and her pulse is scarcely to be felt."

A weight was taken off me; I was instinctively certain that my darling was saved.

"Laura," I said, "this is not bad news; provided the flooding has ceased entirely, all that is necessary is to give her some light food."

"A physician has been sent for. He will prescribe whatever is right, but to tell you the truth I have not much hope."

"Only give me the assurance that she is still alive."

"Yes, she is, I assure you; but you understand very well that she will not tell the truth to the doctor, and God knows what he will order. I whispered to her not to take anything, and she understood me."

"You are the best of women. Yes, if she does not die from weakness before to-morrow, she is saved; nature and love will have been her doctors."

"May God hear you! I shall be back by twelve."

"Why not before?"

"Because her room will be full of people."

Feeling the need of hope, and almost dead for want of food, I ordered some dinner, and prepared a long letter for my beloved mistress, to be delivered to her when she was well enough to read it. The instants given to repentance are very sad, and I was truly a fit subject for pity. I longed to see Laura again, so as to hear what the doctor had said. I had very good cause for laughing at all sorts of oracles, yet through some unaccountable weakness I longed for that of the doctor; I wanted, before all, to find it a propitious one.

Laura's young daughters waited upon me at dinner; I could not manage to swallow a mouthful, but it amused me to see the three sisters devour my dinner at the first invitation I gave them. The eldest sister, a very fine girl, never raised her large eyes once towards me. The two younger ones seemed to me disposed to be amiable, but if I looked at them it was only to feed my despair and the cruel pangs of repentance.

At last Laura, whom I expected anxiously, came back; she told me that the dear patient remained in the same state of debility; the doctor had been greatly puzzled by her extreme weakness because he did not know to what cause to attribute it. Laura added,

"He has ordered some restoratives and a small quantity of light broth; if she can sleep, he answers for her life. He has likewise desired her to have someone to watch her at night, and she immediately pointed her finger at me, as if she wished me to undertake that office. Now, I promise you never to leave her either night or day, except to bring you news."

I thanked her, assuring her that I would reward her generously. I heard with great pleasure that her mother had paid her a visit, and that she had no suspicion of the real state of things, for she had lavished on her the most tender caresses.

Feeling more at ease I gave six sequins to Laura, one to each of her daughters, and ate something for my supper: I then laid myself down on one of the wretched beds in the room. As soon as the two younger sisters saw me in bed, they undressed themselves without ceremony, and took possession of the second bed which was close by mine. Their innocent confidence pleased me. The eldest sister, who most likely had more practical experience, retired to the adjoining room; she had a lover to whom she was soon to be married. This time, however, I was not possessed with the evil spirit of concupiscence, and I allowed innocence to sleep peacefully without attempting anything against it.

Early the next morning Laura was the bearer of good news. She came in with a cheerful air to announce that the beloved patient had slept well, and that she was going back soon to give her some soup. I felt an almost maddening joy in listening to her, and I thought the oracle of Aesculapius a thousand times more reliable than that of Apollo. But it was not yet time to exult in our victory, for my poor little friend had to recover her strength and to make up for all the blood she had lost; that could be done only by time and careful nursing. I remained another week at Laura's house, which I left only after my dear C— C— had requested me to do so in a letter of four pages. Laura, when I left, wept for joy in seeing herself rewarded by the gift of all the fine linen I had bought for my C— C—, and her daughters were weeping likewise, most probably because, during the ten days I had spent near them, they had not obtained a single kiss from me.

After my return to Venice, I resumed my usual habits; but with a nature like mine how could I possibly remain satisfied without positive love? My only pleasure was to receive a letter from my dear recluse every Wednesday, who advised me to wait patiently rather than to attempt carrying her off. Laura assured me that she had become more lovely than ever, and I longed to see her. An opportunity of gratifying my wishes soon offered itself, and I did not allow it to escape. There was to be a taking of the veil—a ceremony which always attracts a large number of persons. On those occasions the nuns always received a great many visitors, and I thought that the boarders were likely to be in the parlour on such an occasion. I ran no risk of being remarked any more than any other person, for I would mingle with the crowd. I therefore went without saying anything about it to Laura, and without acquainting my dear little wife of my intentions. I thought I would fall, so great was my emotion, when I saw her within four yards from me, and looking at me as if she had been in an ecstatic state. I thought her taller and more womanly, and she certainly seemed to me more beautiful than before. I saw no one but her; she never took her eyes off me, and I was the last to leave that place which on that day struck me as being the temple of happiness.

Three days afterwards I received a letter from her. She painted with such vivid colours the happiness she had felt in seeing me, that I made up my mind to give her that pleasure as often as I could. I answered at once that I would attend mass every Sunday at the church of her convent. It cost me nothing: I could not see her, but I knew that she saw me herself, and her happiness made me perfectly happy. I had nothing to fear, for it was almost impossible that anyone could recognize me in the church which was attended only by the people of Muran.

After hearing two or three masses, I used to take a gondola, the gondolier of which could not feel any curiosity about me. Yet I kept on my guard, for I knew that the father of C— C— wanted her to forget me, and I had no doubt he would have taken her away, God knew where if he had had the slightest suspicion of my being acquainted with the place where he had confined her.

Thus I was reasoning in my fear to lose all opportunity of corresponding with my dear C— C—, but I did not yet know the disposition and the shrewdness of the sainted daughters of the Lord. I did not suppose that there was anything remarkable in my person, at least for the inmates of a convent; but I was yet a novice respecting the curiosity of women, and particularly of unoccupied hearts; I had soon occasion to be convinced.

I had executed my Sunday manoeuvering only for a month or five weeks, when my dear C— C— wrote me jestingly that I had become a living enigma for all the convent, boarders and nuns, not even excepting the old ones. They all expected me anxiously; they warned each other of my arrival, and watched me taking the holy water. They remarked that I never cast a glance toward the grating, behind which were all the inmates of the convent; that I never looked at any of the women coming in or going out of the church. The old nuns said that I was certainly labouring under some deep sorrow, of which I had no hope to be cured except through the protection of the Holy Virgin, and the young ones asserted that I was either melancholy or misanthropic.

My dear wife, who knew better than the others, and had no occasion to lose herself in suppositions, was much amused, and she entertained me by sending me a faithful report of it all. I wrote to her that, if she had any fear of my being recognized I would cease my Sunday visits to the church. She answered that I could not impose upon her a more cruel privation, and she entreated me to continue my visits. I thought it would be prudent, however, to abstain from calling at Laura's house, for fear of the chattering nuns contriving to know it, and discovering in that manner a great deal more than I wished them to find out. But that existence was literally consuming me by slow degrees, and could not last long. Besides, I was made to have a mistress, and to live happily with her. Not knowing what to do with myself, I would gamble, and I almost invariably won; but, in spite of that, weariness had got hold of me and I was getting thinner every day.

With the five thousand sequins which my partner Croce had won for me in Padua I had followed M. Bragadin's advice. I had hired a casino where I held a faro bank in partnership with a matador, who secured me against the frauds of certain noblemen—tyrants, with whom a private citizen is always sure to be in the wrong in my dear country.

On All Saints' Day, in the year 1753, just as, after hearing mass, I was going to step into a gondola to return to Venice, I saw a woman, somewhat in Laura's style who, passing near me, looked at me and dropped a letter. I picked it up, and the woman, seeing me in possession of the epistle, quietly went on. The letter had no address, and the seal represented a running knot. I stepped hurriedly into the gondola, and as soon as we were in the offing I broke the seal. I read the following words.

"A nun, who for the last two months and a half has seen you every Sunday in the church of her convent, wishes to become acquainted with you. A pamphlet which you have lost, and which chance has thrown into her hands, makes her believe that you speak French; but, if you like it better, you can answer in Italian, because what she wants above all is a clear and precise answer. She does not invite you to call for her at the parlour of the convent, because, before you place yourself under the necessity of speaking to her, she wishes you to see her, and for that purpose she will name a lady whom you can accompany to the parlour. That lady shall not know you and need not therefore introduce you, in case you should not wish to be known.

"Should you not approve of that way to become acquainted, the nun will appoint a certain casino in Muran, in which you will find her alone, in the evening, any night you may choose. You will then be at liberty either to sup with her, or to retire after an interview of a quarter of an hour, if you have any other engagements.

"Would you rather offer her a supper in Venice? Name the night, the hour, the place of appointment, and you will see her come out of a gondola. Only be careful to be there alone, masked and with a lantern.

"I feel certain that you will answer me, and that you will guess how impatiently I am waiting for your letter. I entreat you, therefore, to give it to-morrow to the same woman through whom you will receive mine! you will find her one hour before noon in the church of St. Cancian, near the first altar on the right.

"Recollect that, if I did not suppose you endowed with a noble soul and a high mind, I could never have resolved on taking a step which might give you an unfavorable opinion of my character."

The tone of that letter, which I have copied word by word, surprised me even more than the offer it contained. I had business to attend to, but I gave up all engagements to lock myself in my room in order to answer it. Such an application betokened an extravagant mind, but there was in it a certain dignity, a singularity, which attracted me. I had an idea that the writer might be the same nun who taught French to C— C—. She had represented her friend in her letters as handsome, rich, gallant, and generous. My dear wife had, perhaps, been guilty of some indiscretion. A thousand fancies whirled through my brain, but I would entertain only those which were favourable to a scheme highly pleasing to me. Besides, my young friend had informed me that the nun who had given her French lessons was not the only one in the convent who spoke that language. I had no reason to suppose that, if C— C— had made a confidante of her friend, she would have made a mystery of it to me. But, for all that, the nun who had written to me might be the beautiful friend of my dear little wife, and she might also turn out to be a different person; I felt somewhat puzzled. Here is, however, the letter which I thought I could write without implicating myself:

"I answer in French, madam, in the hope that my letter will have the clearness and the precision of which you give me the example in yours.

"The subject is highly interesting and of the highest importance, considering all the circumstances. As I must answer without knowing the person to whom I am writing, you must feel, madam, that, unless I should possess a large dose of vanity, I must fear some mystification, and my honour requires that I should keep on my guard.

"If it is true that the person who has penned that letter is a respectable woman, who renders me justice in supposing me endowed with feeling as noble as her own, she will find, I trust, that I could not answer in any other way than I am doing now.

"If you have judged me worthy, madam, of the honour which you do me by offering me your acquaintance, although your good opinion can have been formed only from my personal appearance, I feel it my duty to obey you, even if the result be to undeceive you by proving that I had unwittingly led you into a mistaken appreciation of my person.

"Of the three proposals which you so kindly made in your letter, I dare not accept any but the first, with the restriction suggested by your penetrating mind. I will accompany to the parlour of your convent a lady who shall not know who I am, and, consequently, shall have no occasion to introduce me.

"Do not judge too severely, madam, the specious reasons which compel me not to give you my name, and receive my word of honour that I shall learn yours only to render you homage. If you choose to speak to me, I will answer with the most profound respect. Permit me to hope that you will come to the parlour alone. I may mention that I am a Venetian, and perfectly free.

"The only reason which prevents me from choosing one of the two other arrangements proposed by you, either of which would have suited me better because they greatly honour me, is, allow me to repeat it, a fear of being the victim of a mystification; but these modes of meeting will not be lost when you know me and when I have seen you. I entreat you to have faith in my honour, and to measure my patience by your own. Tomorrow, at the same place and at the same hour, I shall be anxiously expecting your answer."

I went to the place appointed, and having met the female Mercury I gave her my letter with a sequin, and I told her that I would come the next day for the answer. We were both punctual. As soon as she saw me, she handed me back the sequin which I had given her the day before, and a letter, requesting me to read it and to let her know whether she was to wait for an answer. Here is the exact copy of the letter:

"I believe, sir, that I have not been mistaken in anything. Like you, I detest untruth when it can lead to important consequences, but I think it a mere trifle when it can do no injury to anyone. Of my three proposals you have chosen the one which does the greatest honour to your intelligence, and, respecting the reasons which induce you to keep your incognito, I have written the enclosed to the Countess of S—, which I request you to read. Be kind enough to seal it before delivery of it to her. You may call upon her whenever convenient to yourself. She will name her own hour, and you will accompany her here in her gondola. The countess will not ask you any questions, and you need not give her any explanation. There will be no presentation; but as you will be made acquainted with my name, you can afterwards call on me here, masked, whenever you please, and by using the name of the countess. In that way we shall become acquainted without the necessity of disturbing you, or of your losing at night some hours which may be precious to you. I have instructed my servant to wait for your answer in case you should be known to the countess and object to her. If you approve of the choice I have made of her, tell the messenger that there is no answer."

As I was an entire stranger to the countess, I told the woman that I had no answer to give, and she left me.

Here are the contents of the note addressed by the nun to the countess, and which I had to deliver to her:

"I beg of you, my dear friend, to pay me a visit when you are at leisure, and to let the masked gentleman-bearer of this note know the hour, so that he can accompany you. He will be punctual. Farewell. You will much oblige your friend."

That letter seemed to me informed by a sublime spirit of intrigue; there was in it an appearance of dignity which captivated me, although I felt conscious that I was playing the character of a man on whom a favour seemed to be bestowed.

In her last letter, my nun, pretending not to be anxious to know who I was, approved of my choice, and feigned indifference for nocturnal meetings; but she seemed certain that after seeing her I would visit her. I knew very well what to think of it all, for the intrigue was sure to have an amorous issue. Nevertheless, her assurance, or rather confidence, increased my curiosity, and I felt that she had every reason to hope, if she were young and handsome. I might very well have delayed the affair for a few days, and have learned from C— C— who that nun could be; but, besides the baseness of such a proceeding, I was afraid of spoiling the game and repenting it afterwards. I was told to call on the countess at my convenience, but it was because the dignity of my nun would not allow her to shew herself too impatient; and she certainly thought that I would myself hasten the adventure. She seemed to me too deeply learned in gallantry to admit the possibility of her being an inexperienced novice, and I was afraid of wasting my time; but I made up my mind to laugh at my own expense if I happened to meet a superannuated female. It is very certain that if I had not been actuated by curiosity I should not have gone one step further, but I wanted to see the countenance of a nun who had offered to come to Venice to sup with me. Besides, I was much surprised at the liberty enjoyed by those sainted virgins, and at the facility with which they could escape out of their walls.

At three o'clock I presented myself before the countess and delivered the note, and she expressed a wish to see me the next day at the same hour. We dropped a beautiful reverence to one another, and parted. She was a superior woman, already going down the hill, but still very handsome.

The next morning, being Sunday, I need not say that I took care to attend mass at the convent, elegantly dressed, and already unfaithful—at least in idea—to my dear C— C—, for I was thinking of being seen by the nun, young or old, rather than of shewing myself to my charming wife.

In the afternoon I masked myself again, and at the appointed time I repaired to the house of the countess who was waiting for me. We went in a two-oared gondola, and reached the convent without having spoken of anything but the weather. When we arrived at the gate, the countess asked for M— M—. I was surprised by that name, for the woman to whom it belonged was celebrated. We were shewn into a small parlour, and a few minutes afterwards a nun came in, went straight to the grating, touched a spring, and made four squares of the grating revolve, which left an opening sufficiently large to enable the two friends to embrace the ingenious window was afterwards carefully closed. The opening was at least eighteen inches wide, and a man of my size could easily have got through it. The countess sat opposite the nun, and I took my seat a little on one side so as to be able to observe quietly and at my ease one of the most beautiful women that it was possible to see. I had no doubt whatever of her being the person mentioned by my dear C— C— as teaching her French. Admiration kept me in a sort of ecstacy, and I never heard one word of their conversation; the beautiful nun, far from speaking to me, did not even condescend to honour me with one look. She was about twenty-two or twenty-three years of age, and the shape of her face was most beautiful. Her figure was much above the ordinary height, her complexion rather pale, her appearance noble, full of energy, but at the same time reserved and

GIACOMO CASANOVA

modest; her eyes, large and full, were of a lovely blue; her countenance was soft and cheerful; her fine lips seemed to breathe the most heavenly voluptuousness, and her teeth were two rows of the most brilliant enamel. Her head-dress did not allow me to see her hair, but if she had any I knew by the colour of her eyebrows that it was of a beautiful light brown. Her hand and her arm, which I could see as far as the elbow, were magnificent; the chisel of Praxiteles never carved anything more grace fully rounded and plump, I was not sorry to have refused the two rendezvous which had been offered to me by the beauty, for I was sure of possessing her in a few days, and it was a pleasure for me to lay my desires at her feet. I longed to find myself alone with her near that grating, and I would have considered it an insult to her if, the very next day, I had not come to tell her how fully I rendered to her charms the justice they deserved. She was faithful to her determination not to look at me once, but after all I was pleased with her reserve. All at once the two friends lowered their voices, and out of delicacy I withdrew further. Their private conversation lasted about a quarter of an hour, during which I pretended to be intently looking at a painting; then they kissed one another again by the same process as at the beginning of the interview; the nun closed the opening, turned her back on us, and disappeared without casting one glance in my direction.

As we were on our way back to Venice, the countess, tired perhaps of our silence, said to me, with a smile,

"M— M— is beautiful and very witty."

"I have seen her beauty, and I believe in her wit."

"She did not address one word to you."

"I had refused to be introduced to her, and she punished me by pretending not to know that I was present."

The countess made no answer, and we reached her house without exchanging another word. At her door a very ceremonious curtesy, with these words, "Adieu, sir!" warned me that I was not to go any further. I had no wish to do so, and went away dreaming and wondering at the singularity of the adventure, the end of which I longed to see.

Note About the Author

Giacomo Casanova (1725–1798) was an Italian adventurer and author. Born in Venice, Casanova was the eldest of six siblings born to Gaetano Casanova and Zanetta Farussi, an actor and actress. Raised in a city noted for its cosmopolitanism, night life, and glamor, Casanova overcame a sickly childhood to excel in school, entering the University of Padua at the age of 12. After graduating in 1742 with a degree in law, he struggled to balance his work as a lawyer and low-level cleric with a growing gambling addiction. As scandals and a prison sentence threatened to derail his career in the church, Casanova managed to find work as a scribe for a powerful Cardinal in Rome, but was soon dismissed and entered military service for the Republic of Venice. Over the next several years, he left the service, succeeded as a professional gambler, and embarked on a Grand Tour of Europe. Towards the end of his life, Casanova worked on his exhaustive, scandalous memoirs, a 12-volume autobiography reflecting on a legendary life of romance and debauchery that brought him from the heights of aristocratic society to the lows of illness and imprisonment. Recognized for his self-styled sensationalism as much as he is for his detailed chronicling of 18th century European culture, Casanova is a man whose name is now synonymous with the kind of life he led—fast, fearless, and free.

A Note from the Publisher

Spanning many genres, from non-fiction essays to literature classics to children's books and lyric poetry, Mint Edition books showcase the master works of our time in a modern new package. The text is freshly typeset, is clean and easy to read, and features a new note about the author in each volume. Many books also include exclusive new introductory material. Every book boasts a striking new cover, which makes it as appropriate for collecting as it is for gift giving. Mint Edition books are only printed when a reader orders them, so natural resources are not wasted. We're proud that our books are never manufactured in excess and exist only in the exact quantity they need to be read and enjoyed.

bookfinity™

Discover more of your favorite classics with Bookfinity™.

- Track your reading with custom book lists.
- Get great book recommendations for your personalized Reader Type.
- Add reviews for your favorite books.
- AND MUCH MORE!

Visit **bookfinity.com** and take the fun Reader Type quiz to get started.

Enjoy our classic and modern companion pairings!

Classic & Modern